DO YOU KNOW . . .

* how it's bad business to invest in a tract house?

* how to become a financial individualist and avoid slick salesmen?

* how to refinance a mortgage at lower interest rates?

* how to protect yourself from the financial and political dangers of inflation?

* how to save money and make money when fixing up property?

* real estate "tricks" to enhance your property?

* the problems and pitfalls of successful negotiation?

* how to prevent the erosion and skimming of your estate after death?

* whether and when to rent or sell your property?

What You *Don't* Know Can Cost A Fortune You Don't Have.

What You *Do* Know Can *Make That Fortune*—If You're Big Enough To Handle It!

HOW TO MAKE MONEY FAST SPECULATING IN DISTRESSED PROPERTY

John V. Kamin
Consulting Economist

Forecaster Publishing Co., Inc.
Tarzana, CA 91356

HOW TO MAKE MONEY FAST SPECULATING IN
DISTRESSED PROPERTY

A FORECASTER BOOK

Third Edition, 1977

ISBN 0-515-03102-X

FORECASTER books are published by FORECASTER
Publishing Co., Inc. Its trademarks, consisting of
the words "The FORECASTER" and the portrayal
thereof, are registered in the United States Patent
Office

FORECASTER PUBLISHING CO., INC.
19623 Ventura Boulevard
Tarzana, California 91356

TABLE OF CONTENTS

FOREWORD
Illusion of Ownership

Everyone likes to think that he OWNS things. People like to think they own land, buildings, stocks, possessions ... and sometimes, other people. But when you consider this attitude of ownership over the long term, it has to be erroneous. Nobody owns any hard assets. They are merely TEMPORARY CUSTODIANS of items of value.

Take the land you are standing on, for example. You may think you own it, or somebody else owns it. Not so! Seventy-five years from now, it will be registered in the name of someone who is not yet born. Five hundred years from now, who knows who will "own" it? Seventy-five years ago, a bunch of Indians probably thought they were the owners. Four or five centuries ago, a Spanish king thought he was the owner. And a few thousand years ago, some Macedonian, called Alexander, thought he owned it all. He lived to the ripe old age of 28.

Ownership, as we normally think of it, is nothing but an illusion. We are merely temporary custodians of items thought to be of value during our lifetime. Rare coins or paintings are other examples. If you think they will still be in your family, under your ownership, 200 years from now, you are sadly mistaken. The odds are 100 to 1 against it. You merely have them in your temporary custody to enjoy and to hold, hopefully while the value rises.

INTRODUCTION

Can you visualize what the folded wad of one hundred $100 bills looks like? Can you see yourself stuffing them, forcing them into your own pocket - with the outside bills being crumpled in the process?

The purpose of this book is to enable you to create money, money you would not have had if you had not encountered and read this book.

It is very important that you be able to visualize yourself with a lot of cash. If you cannot visualize it, you probably have some mental roadblocks and are not ready to read these concepts and act upon them successfully.

If you CAN visualize yourself with a lot of money, a hundred $100 bills, you will find that such continual visualization brings all sorts of good qualities, necessary for your success, into play - qualities such as bulldog determination, the enthusiasm to go the extra mile, the ability to overcome and surmount obstacles, including people's continual discouragement of your present and potential achievements. That is WHY this book was written.

This is a report on speculation. It is not concerned with INVESTMENT in real estate. In fact, there is no such thing as investment - all money generation is the result of either speculation or gambling. This book is not about income property, properties calculated to yield you so many percent per year. It's about making CHUNKS of money - not little dribs and drabs!

This book is for non-real estate people, people with other occupations. It is for folks who sometimes might get the feeling that they are wage slaves, for all who are not independently wealthy. It is for those

11

who may not be in a position to leave their present occupation right now but would like to do so eventually, to become financially independent and engage in work BY CHOICE, not by necessity.

It is for young people in their late teens and twenties who do not wish to work for 45 years to get a gold watch. It is for people in their thirties and forties who are working hard but don't seem to be getting anywhere. It is for people in their fifties and up who have accumulated many experiences and some wisdom, but who have not quite yet been able to "put it all together" in a manner that yields them chunks of money.

This book tries to help you make money in a reasonable period of time, normally one to five year holding periods. And as you get into speculation, you may discover the profit process can be speeded up, sometimes to holding periods of less than a year.

Over 90% of the ever-expanding American population lives on 1% of the land. This book deals with getting some of that 90% to bid for land you hold in adjacent areas.

Chapter 1

WHY REAL ESTATE?

There is a friendly debate going on concerning
the wisdom of buying real estate in today's present
economic circumstances, in attempts to make short-
term and long-term speculative profits. Most seem
to be directly opposed to buying real estate for profits
at this juncture. Some are advising their clients to
sell what they have. "Don't touch it," they say.

The debate brings out some interesting points
regarding your ability to make thousands of dollars
and speculative profits in the near future in real estate. Can it be done? Can you do it? What stands in
your way?

The real estate "knockers" cite the danger of a
recession or a world-wide depression. Some believe
that we are already moving toward a world-wide depression, perhaps to occur within a few months.
Other real estate detractors specify the disorder in
the currency markets. "The dollar is in great danger and people are not willing to make long-term
commitments," they say. "Monetary chaos and
further turmoil will reign supreme." Another school
of real estate detractors cites continually rising taxes
on property. "Property taxes are rising and are becoming unbelievable," they say. Furthermore, they
see the rising taxes as a continuing trend. Another
good reason many of the detractors don't like real estate is the possibility of wage-price-rent controls.
"How can you count on continued net rental income
when rents are frozen and taxes and maintenance
costs are rising?" they ask.

These are all very good points, positions that
those in favor of avoiding real estate or selling out

have brought up. Their four main reasons for avoiding real estate boil down to (a) fear of a recession or depression, (b) watered currencies, money pollution, financing turmoil, (c) continually rising property taxation trends, and (d) rent controls. Under normal circumstances any one or two of these reasons would be good reason for avoiding real estate or selling out, wouldn't they? The line-up of four reasons, all at the same time, seems to make a good case against owning or buying any real estate at this time. Or does it?

Since (a), fear of a depression, seems to be the strongest and most valid reason for fearing any real estate commitments, let's deal with that one first:

Is it too early to use real estate as a vehicle? Are we on the verge of a depression? If depression looms, will prices fall as in 1932? Past decades present a sorry picture of thousands of promises that inflation was controlled, halted, and nonexistent. Now, one is faced with the prospect that even this sorry historical picture may be exceeded by even greater erosion of purchasing power over the coming decades. Fixed-income instruments (paper assets), therefore, will play a decreasing role in any investment plans. The necessity of owning SOMETHING in the way of hard assets should be made clear to everyone, particularly those of the younger generation who seem to have an unjustified faith that government has the ability to violate natural economic laws at will. If money could be created and if its value could be legislated by printing currency, then Brazil, Chile, Vietnam and India would be among the richest nations of the world.

We should consider the possibility that the government may soon print money as never before - another flood of PRINTING PRESS MONEY! This fact puts you in a somewhat different position than the real estate investors in 1931 or 1932. At that time,

printing press money was not a factor. Nor was
there a need for 30 million dwelling units in the next
few years. People were not so concentrated in the
big cities and the population was only a fraction of
the present size. Today all those conditions have
changed. People will continue to move out from city
centers. They are being forced out by conditions beyond their control, by a changing environment, and
by rapacious city taxes. Gas price increases will not
halt the forward march to suburbia.

The way to make money in real estate is to buy
low and to sell high. We have already been in reces-
sions every few years in the national economy as far
as real estate is concerned. As far as a recession
in the real estate market is concerned, you are already there!! There is no guarantee that prices
won't decline further. They may. You can limit
your risk against further declines by buying real estate 20% to 40% below current market levels. Therefore, even if prices should fall another 20% to 40%,
your risk factor would be minimum.

You may not catch the exact bottom of the market,
but by buying in the next few months you will certainly
be buying way under the top. There is no way to take
all the risk out of real estate, but by buying during
recession-depression periods, and buying when many
of the regular real estate investors are scared of it,
you can buy way down from the highs. Buying way
down from the highs places the risk burden elsewhere
- not on you.

Aristotle Onassis made a great fortune buying
surplus ships and tankers when no one else would have
them after the war. And wasn't it one of the Rothschilds
who said, "Buy when the blood is running in the
streets!"? If your strategy in any investment deal
is to avoid buying at the higher point, and to make
commitments during the low points of certain specific
cycles, surely you must be at or near such a time
period right now in real estate.

(b) Fear of owning real estate because of currency turmoil, money pollution, financing problems:
These are valid reasons for buying real estate now,
rather than waiting. These are not reasons for not
buying real estate. Right now financing is still easy
on real estate. It might not be nearly so easy to get
in the future. In fact, during a prolonged period of
money pollution - a la Brazil, real estate turns out
to be one of the only protections; as an example, witness the rows and rows of temporarily vacant apartments standing in Brazil, built as a continuing refuge
against constantly devaluing currency. If you finance
70% to 90% of your real estate purchase now on a
long-term loan, and the currency continues being
watered, you will pay off that lender in scrip of less
purchasing power.

The idea is to keep most of your capital intact
for your own use and protection - and tie up only
small amounts of your net worth in real estate,
financing the rest. In times such as these approximately 40% of your net worth (assuming your net
worth is $100,000 or more), should be in a relatively
liquid position. The only real estate you want to
hold outright is your home. The rest should all be
heavily hocked (financed).

(c) Continually rising property-tax trend: On the
surface this presents a very good reason for avoiding
real estate. Taxes can only rise as properties are
appraised higher. Furthermore, there is a significant
time lag. The market recognizes increases in property values faster than the property-tax authorities.
That always gives you an edge on selling for higher
prices. Furthermore, continually rising taxes mean
that property values rise far above amounts financed.
Again - the opportunity to pay off lenders' loans in
shrinking dollars.

Current taxes are an important factor in figuring
rentals that can be charged. Higher appraisals mean

profits rather than losses. Like currency pollution, it is a factor that works for you – not against you. The spectre of rising taxes will be covered more in the following paragraphs.

(d) Rent controls: True, rents can be frozen. Therefore, income generated from properties could be frozen. For people seeking current income, their hands could be tied. But there is far more to consider than current income when you evaluate the merits of speculating in real estate right now. First, the wage-price controls may be imposed at least temporarily, off and on. When they are lifted that will be an opportunity to raise rents sharply, hence raising rental income.

Second, when you buy real estate you should focus your attention on capital gains, not income. You are in to make a lot of money, not small 8% or 9% returns. Your reason for speculating is to make minimum chunks of $5,000 or more at a time. Should the lid come off on rent controls and you raise the rent on property you already own, you can sell that property for much more money.

What if the lid on rent controls never comes off? What if you are hung with rent controls on rentable property for several years? Good question. For the answer, look at the following Econometric Chart. As supplies fail to keep pace (because of artificially suppressed prices), with rental space demanded (by those who are willing to pay a higher price to get what they want, blackmarkets and shortages develop. Under-the-table payments become commonplace. Potential renters turn into buyers; they kick out the present tenants and take over the building for their own use. You saw it happen in World War II. When shortages and blackmarkets like these develop, you can sell buildings at much higher prices than frozen rentals would indicate. Potential renters are suddenly willing to become buyers, just so they can get the space they need.

It is probably very difficult for the average person to envision a shortage of real estate or automobiles or anything else at this time as a direct result of wage-price-rent controls. Yet, if they are left on for any lengthy period of time, you can bet your bottom buck that shortages and blackmarkets will appear. Furthermore, they will appear a lot faster than during World War II for this time there is no "patriotic" effort, or "our boys dying over there" kind of appeal. If wage-price-rent controls are left on for any lengthy period of time, the majority of the population will engage in the blackmarkets and quasi-criminal activities (just as British citizens, who regularly traveled abroad, engaged in illegal activity when currency controls were in effect during the late 1960's).

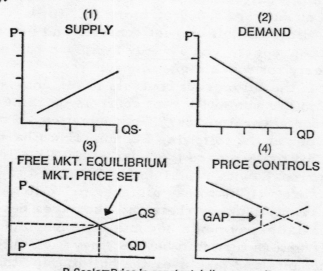

P-Scale=Price in constant dollars per unit
Q-Scale=Quantity
QS=Quantity supplied or produced
QD=Quantity demanded by consumers
GAP=Eventual shortages or blackmarkets

ECONOMETRIC CHART

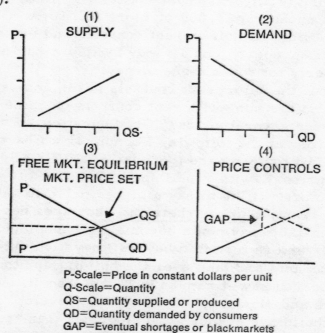

18

Under price-rent controls, the supply side on the chart halts early. Producers of suppressed-price goods, are willing to supply only limited quantities in the marketplace. Therefore, suppressed prices soon result in suppressed quantities produced, quantities insufficient to meet the demand. Demanders are willing to pay higher prices so they go through the blackmarket or make under-the-table payments, or do something to get the job done. Either they pay, or they do without! This is particularly true of businessmen needing new or expanded facilities for their business.

HOUSING SHORTAGE

The residential housing industry has been in trouble for 12 straight years. Most of the industry leaders have a black outlook right about now. Yet, the housing industry may be a most optimistic area in which to consider placing funds. It appears to be at the bottom of its normal cycle, or very near there.

Within 36 months we will be in the midst of a housing demand unequalled since Korea. We have had relatively tight money now for nigh on to 7 years. The average house payment is probably up some 70% during that period due mainly to higher labor costs, material costs, and higher money-rental costs.

Needless to say, during this period buyers have not exactly been falling all over themselves to purchase. Go back to 1964, when almost anything that had a roof and four walls would sell easily, and you discover that compared to 1964, present new house sales have made a poor showing. Used housing continues to sell well.

The rate of family formations has stabilized its trend now, after several years of decline. So have birth rates. Latent housing demand is also likely to come, to some extent, from the servicemen returning from Thailand, Korea, and Germany. In addition, huge areas of the central cities are turning into uninhabitable, heavy-taxed jungles! Wage earners, by their move out of city cores, are turning central city housing obsolete at a faster pace than at any time we can remember. The run to the suburbs by individuals of all groups, and industry, is continuing to accelerate. This tremendous housing demand that is building up, and that will continue to build up, will probably not be satisfied for many years.

And in spite of the substantial amount of vacant land in the U.S.A. today, the supply of useable, buildable property, with utilities, within commuting distance of major metro centers, is definitely limited. When residential building jumps 50% and 100% a few years from now, builders will have to have the land. Your land!

NOW IS THE TIME TO BUY

Residential construction prices may rise 10% in the next 15 months. This is probably the best time and the finest opportunity in the past three years to make a purchase below market. Interest rates have eased off and mortgage money is once again readily available, especially since savings and loans now have a little monetary inflow. At the same time, you are in a very strong negotiating position since lots of properties are going into foreclosure with the rise in unemployment.

Our latest recession is different from past ones in that unemployment has hit the skilled worker and the semi-professional man hard. For example, in California, it is not the laborer or steno who is unemployed. It is the aerospace engineer. Many are not willing to switch their profession or their industry; they are completely inflexible and immobile, and their unemployment benefits are running out. What do you do with an engineer who won't move and won't learn a new line?

In the $45,000 to $85,000 class particularly, there are many residences that can be bought a full $10,000 less than what they sold for last year. Some have underlined assumable loans at a much lower interest rate. The field is ripe for the picking.

This is not to say that everyone is going to get rich buying residential real estate; it is a tough game. If you are going to buy a medium or high-priced house, however, you could not find a better time to do so. On the other hand, there do not seem to be many bargains in tract houses of new developments. Take a look at the Econometric Chart.

Now, note how the average purchase price increased most sharply on existing homes, much faster than on new homes, between 1964 and 1976. The average transaction price on existing homes on chart (Pg. 22) has increased more than 50% faster on brand new homes. Look for a great many surprises in residences five years old and more in nice established suburban neighborhoods if you need a good place to live. With a little exertion on your part and a few calls to your friendly lenders, you will have the opportunity of the decade to buy a residence at a favorable price. If you are an inner-city resident and plan to make a move to suburbia eventually, now is your chance. This is the time to get into action. There are some excellent buys around just now with mortgage rates a full 1% to 3% below their earlier highs.

SALE PRICES OF HOMES

YEAR	USED (EXISTING) MEDIAN	AVERAGE	NEW MEDIAN	AVERAGE
1966	$18,800	$20,600	$21,400	$23,300
1967	19,400	21,600	22,700	24,600
1968	20,100	22,300	24,700	26,600
1969	21,800	23,700	25,600	27,900
1970	23,000	25,700	23,400	26,600
1971	24,800	28,000	25,200	28,300
1972	26,700	30,100	27,600	30,500
1973	28,900	32,900	32,500	35,500
1974	32,000	35,800	35,900	38,900
1975	35,300	39,000	39,300	42,600
September 1, 1976	38,700	42,700	44,800	-----

22

Chapter 2

WHO SHOULD INVEST?

All of us are born financial slaves. For many long years we are completely dependent on others for food, clothing, shelter, education, etc. Many folks enter their adult lives taking on a never-ending barrage of monthly payments. Suddenly they discover they are 50 and the monthly payments are taking the same percentage of their monthly income as when they were 25.

With planning, this doesn't have to happen! Read the following examples. Do they apply to you?

During 1968 and 1969, many young families tried to build capital for a period of one or two years. Many moved from heavily over-extended positions to positions where most of their debts were paid off and they even managed to save a few thousand dollars. Suddenly they found themselves in an alien culture. While they had made progress, all their friends, relatives and associates remained heavily over-extended. Nowhere except in a few publications did they read of the benefits of being free of debt. All of their friends pooh-poohed the idea and told these young families they were foolish to mess around becoming financially secure.

At this point, many who had tried to build liquidity, to build capital, suddenly became easy prey for slick-talking salesmen. Perhaps it was a tract-house pusher, perhaps the color TV dealer. Every salesman makes the successful family feel they are on the wrong track – when the family refuses to take on additional debt burdens. Sometimes the salesman will go so far as to laugh at them. By these psychological tactics some individuals and families are again convinced to rejoin the ranks of financial weaklings - after a short membership in the Financial Freedom Club!

Our entire culture prepares folks to be debtors so they can be manipulated and easily controlled. However, after the first flush of success, a few families will actually LIKE the idea of being debt-free. What mavericks! These folks will realize they stand at the point of decision now, a point where they can choose a road that will free them forever from monthly payments for the rest of their lives!

For example, if these few folks who choose freedom from debt need a house, they will not choose the tract-house route with the $400 per month payments. Instead, they will search hard and long for a deal where they can buy a $30,000 older house in the path of commercial development. They may get $75,000 for it in a few years because someone wants it for a shopping center. Perhaps they will try to scout up a farmhouse in the path of development, with adjacent acreage to resell at a sizeable future profit. Maybe they will buy a triplex, renting the two rentals to pay it off. They will not be deterred by minor obstacles, nor will they be lazy and refuse to spend the time doing the footwork necessary to locate such deals. These folks will soon be on their way to being completely financially independent. They won't fall victims to the slick-talking salesman nor will they go to their obviously over-extended associates for financial advice. Their associates may even be a bit envious when it is apparent what the individualists are doing, and purposely sow doubts in their minds.

Now, when you are out in Texas, or Iowa, or New Jersey, and trying to become a financial individualist, these doubts can sway you from what you know to be the right path. This is a common occurrence. However, if you realize that a $40,000 new house can cost you $90,000 by the time you have it

paid off, you can be more secure in your dealings
with the slick-talking salesmen - and feel confident
in choosing another route.

There is another very interesting tendency.
Some investors will build up a little capital on sound
advice and make a nice capital gain of a few thousand
dollars at the beginning, or maybe put in a few years
of hard saving and accumulate a few thousand. They
then get EXTREMELY nervous. They are not used to
the sudden new security that having a few thousand
liquid capital brings. It begins to worry them. They
are not psychologically prepared to be financially independent in a debtor culture.

These new successes look around, and in their
nervousness, they become superficially interested in
all sorts of wild schemes. None of their friends or
neighbors have anything put by, and they feel some-
how that they are not part of "the group" now. Soon
they ask their friends and neighbors, in a moment of
secrecy, what they should do with the money. That's
like asking the hangman to place the rope. They
grow fearful, edgy, and then - unable to stand it any
longer - they PLUNGE - usually into the worst possible scheme they can find. The newly accumulated
capital quickly vanishes down the rat-hole - GONE!!
Then they give a big secret sigh of relief - knowing
that they no longer have the responsibility of protecting their capital and making it grow. It is gone,
and they are secretly glad! They can now go back to
the financial debt cycle with a new peace of mind,
knowing they will never be able to break it.

All of us have, at one time or another, been disillusioned by friends or associates in a similar manner. The commercial world constantly dangles these
financial temptations before our eyes to some degree.
Yet today, you are at a turning point, a precarious
stage in the business cycle. Which road will you
take? The one to financial freedom? Or the one

that leads to perpetual financial slavery? Many families and individuals may be destroyed in the coming financial upheavals - just as many saw portions of their hard-earned savings destroyed in erratic and unfamiliar markets.

If there were only <u>one</u> message to convey in this book, it would be this: <u>you</u> <u>are</u> <u>not</u> <u>alone!</u> The situations outlined here are commonplace. Society is filled with a population that <u>embraces</u> financial illusions.

OWNING YOUR OWN HOME

One place most folks start in real estate, like it or not, whether they ever progress or not, is in owning their own home. It is a good way to gain experience, but . . . does it make financial sense? Let's examine the mathematics: assume for a moment, you, the wage-earner, have your choice of a $250 per month apartment, or searching about for a real deal on a below-market-price house with payments of $250 per month and small down payment. Which is better for you - the $250 per month mortgage, or the $250 apartment rental?

The first place to look is at your combined federal and state tax bracket. Is it 15%, 25%, 40%? The higher your combined federal and state tax bracket, the more sense it makes to own your own home. This applies particularly to single people since they are usually in a far higher tax bracket as a result of tax discrimination. You will get no tax deductions for your $250 a month apartment. On the other hand, if your combined federal and state tax bracket is 40%, and $225 of your $250 monthly mortgage payment goes for interest and property taxes, you will get a net cash benefit each month of $90, or $1,080 cash in your pocket each year. A yearly thousand-dollar-bill is nothing to sneeze at.

Let's carry the calculation one step further:

suppose, for your $250 monthly mortgage payment you could buy a $32,000 house? Assume that construction costs are going up at roughly 6% per year, your newly purchased house is also going up $1,920 per year. Combine the tax deductions with the increase in value of your home, going up from its present price of $32,000 ($1,920), and you discover you are $3,000 per year better off owning your own home. Suppose, instead, for your $32,000, you step into a house that has a market value of $40,000 to $45,000? Here you stand a chance of making between $8,000 and $13,000 capital gain over and above cash tax benefits and home-owner equity increase.

In other words, for a person in the example mentioned, over a three-year period, he might add in excess of $20,000 to his net worth! In a 36-month period of time! Now, that's worth considering, isn't it?

Another example: What if your combined federal and state tax bracket is only 25%? You would get a direct cash benefit of 25% of $225, $56.25 per month, or $675 per year. Your equity in the home would still increase at the rate of approximately $1,920 per year and, if you bought wisely, you would still stand a chance of an $8,000 to $13,000 capital gain by re-marketing that place some months later. Net result? Slightly lower direct cash benefits on taxes, $660 for one year, or $1,980 for three years, plus full equity increase improving your net worth, plus undiminished chance for capital gain profits. Even with a very low tax bracket in the example illustrated, you could improve your net worth over a three-period of time well in excess of $15,000. Worth considering this simple change in your lifestyle, isn't it?

Owning your own home does give you at least some protection against inflation and monetary mismanagement at the national level. The independent people who are smart enough to understand this would probably also appreciate being independent from the landlord's whim. There is no way you can gain that independence unless <u>you</u> own the property. That <u>vague</u> <u>insecurity</u> is a part of every <u>rental</u> situation.

Chapter 3

THE YOUNG INVESTOR

The young investor has special problems. His capital is very limited and if he is not careful, it may be 10 years before he builds any sizeable amount of speculation money. If he receives anything at all resembling investment advice, it may involve over-touted stocks from a broker who is "broker" than he is. At the same time he is fumbling around in the securities markets, he has the added problems of family responsibilities. Since he is inexperienced in investments, he must also search for an investment area that will "bail him out" if he makes a mistake. In fact, he is lucky to even consider INVESTMENT as a subject for study in his early working years. Surely there must be a better way to go about things!

Let us zero in on the young investor, from 22 to 35, in the hopes of helping him or her to become financially independent. These are the most important years of your life as far as BUILDING CAPITAL is concerned. Come with us to visit two people.

The first is a teach in California's public school system, age 31, single. The man is smart, has an engaging personality, and has been teaching for quite a few years - so he is not on the low end of the pay scale. He has two cars, a fancy foreign one, and an American car several years old. He has his own apartment and has a couple of hundred dollars in savings for an emergency, and plenty of insurance with no cash value. His coin collection, if placed on the market today, would bring about $150 to $250. This young man saw a $20 St. Gaudens gold piece one day which sold then at $80 retail. He wanted it badly. But he would have to struggle and wrestle with his

29

budget for at least several weeks to be able to buy it. He owns no stocks - although he is "thinking about" buying $200 worth of shares. He owns no real estate.

A second young man, same age, three children and a wife, is also teaching in the California school system for a similar number of years at the same salary level. The second man is worth well over a hundred thousand dollars. His net worth is split up among two businesses, securities, paid-for-home, and heavy coin investments. He also has two cars in the family, but both are old enough to have already been depreciated. He intends to take off every third year now from his teaching duties and did so this year. Chances are, even if this man lost his entire net worth, he would soon have it back again because he made most of his investment mistakes early.

Neither of these young men got anything more than "good wishes" from their folks. The first case is not critical, merely typical. The second case is, as you will agree, unusual. For the second man learned early that every $10 he spends during his 20's, is at least $50 in his 40's. In other words, $10 invested in stocks, real estate, coins, or business, becomes, in 25 years, at least $50. Yet, few young people think of their income in this way. The $100 monthly car payment that you send to the finance company in your 20's, is really a $500 bill if wisely invested for two or three decades. Mature investors will agree that these figures are very conservative.

The big trouble with those in their 20's and early 30's seems to be an exaggerated rate of consumption. After all, when you go to school for 12 to 18 years, and perhaps spend a couple of years in the service, by the time you reach 22 or 26 you are absolutely STARVED for consumer goods. These are all those shiny automobiles and fancy vacations, and updated clothes, etc.

Unfortunately, a habit of heavy consumption expenditure during the first years out of school often becomes an unbreakable habit. Soon one has acquired dependents and other obligations and can give little or no thought to a positive investment policy.

There is a way out! Young investors can achieve complete financial independence by the time they reach their 40's, and have the OPTION of continuing to work or not. The principle to remember is to PAY YOURSELF FIRST. If you are a bread-winner, you should be socking away a minimum of 5% to 15% of your total inflow during these years. Single folks should be socking away 25% to 35% of their take-home income. Unfortunately, most just live from payday to payday and from vacation to vacation during these important years. $2,500 put away in your 20's - into coins, good buildable real estate, or securities at market bottoms, can quickly become $10,000 or $20,000. In fact, it is hard to see how, with a little skill and a little luck, you can AVOID becoming financially independent. Even if it is only $10 a week, you should PAY YOURSELF FIRST!

The first man, at age 31, should not be having to struggle with his budget to buy a single $20 gold piece. He should have a minimum of $10,000 speculative capital to play with, and the ability to buy 100 - $20 gold pieces if he so chooses.

The second man was neither particularly lucky nor smart. But he is a hard worker, had the full cooperation of his non-working wife, and tried to see that most of his available funds went into hard investments rather than consumption expenditures.

What about the young person today? Can he afford to buy good, flat, buildable real estate on the fringes of great metropolitan areas? The answer is that he cannot afford to ignore it.

Factory workers and others have made big six-figure capital gains while attending to their familial duties. They have reared families in farm houses on the edge of metropolitan concentrations. They get them cheap (because the houses are old) and buy five to 20 acres of land with them. The one mortgage payment usually costs them little more than if they were to buy a fancier new house, closer in. They realize the possibility of an occasional depression or recession. But they also realize that inflation, printing press money, and population growth would be with us, good business or bad. The debtor is the one who profits most from inflation because his debts become worthless. To be a solvent debtor, you must have good reserves and, at the same time, incur investment debt on assets that will increase in value.

What about folks who are in their twenties but have family obligations during this period of time? You will probably be out looking at houses. You will discover, as most do, that you are faced with the choice of making a purchase or paying rent and piling up rent receipts. You will find also that most new tract houses of medium quality, will run anywhere from $33,000 to $48,000. You should not avoid making a purchase, but avoid purchasing a new tract home.

There is a much better way to build your capital during these most important formative years. Buy a triplex or a fourplex - for the same or a little more, than a tract house. Rent out two or three of the adjacent units, generating sufficient income to make the payments and meet the taxes, and still build up many thousands of dollars in equity capital while you live rent free.

Living in a triplex or a fourplex is not always as nice as living in a new tract house but if you are able to become financially independent you will find your later years blest with other niceties. One of the quirks of the real estate market is that the price of a tract house is determined by the cost of the land, plus the cost of the building, plus a profit for the developer, plus sales. In other words, to over-simplify, the price of a new tract home is mostly determined by its COST.

The price of a triplex or a fourplex is determined in an entirely different manner. It is determined by the income it will generate. The cost of a triplex has very little to do with determining its selling price. Ask any experienced real estate broker. If a triplex nets $700 per month, the selling price or listing price will be determined on the basis of that $700 per month income generated. Replacement costs or orig-inal building costs will be of secondary importance.

Suppose you take this $700 per month triplex and over the next five or six years find that the rent struc-ture of the country changes so that you increase the rents to the $950 monthly level. What has now hap-pened to the value of your triplex? Chances are the selling price has advanced proportionately to the in-crease in rentals. As a very rough guide, you may find that three to four units, well maintained, buildings in fine neighborhoods of less than 10 years of age, will currently sell for $15,000 to $25,000 per unit. Using this scale, a fourplex could be purchased for between $80,000 and $100,000.

Some individuals are bound to bring up the ques-tion of current high interest rates. They will say, "Good heavens, I have to take on a mortgage on which the interest rate is 9%!" However, if the interest rate structure of the country goes down after a few years go by, you will be able to refinance your mortgage at 7% or 8%, or whatever. So today's interest rate, in that instance, would be only a short-term considera-tion. But what if mortgage rates go to 10% or 12% over the next few years? In that case your 9% rate will look very good as well.

Furthermore, the rental structure of the country is determined by many factors: one of these factors is the cost of money and the cost of new construction. Soon, it will cost at least 50% more to construct new apartment buildings. That means the country will have to charge much greater rentals to cover those costs. Your building purchased at today's rental structure will be highly competitive and much more valuable than it is today. It should be quite easy for anyone who studies the situation and shops intelligently for a purchase in today's distressed money markets, to make at least $25,000 over the time period specified, with a down payment of $2,000 to $10,000.

It would be nice if you could be led by the hand through all the various steps of purchasing, financing, and sale - but no endeavor that is highly rewarding is very easy. It will require WORK on your part! It will require study, working capital, and footwork.

Young people just starting out (or now in school) should get out of their metro-center of nativity and home city, their "comfy" rut and TRAVEL. Travel at least one week a year with your eyes open wide. It isn't necessary to spend huge amounts of money. If you are going to choose a place to live, a home, a career, a permanent location, it should not be a CHOICE BY DEFAULT (chosen because you were not exposed to anything else). You should choose the greatest opportunity. As you travel you should be ALERT and try to meet the people in these areas and aggressively search out opportunities (rather than just planing from city to city, hotel room to hotel room). This is one case where the least expensive form of travel is often the most beneficial. It is only in this way that you will be able to COMPARE AND EVALUATE.

Do not be manipulated out of your capital before it reaches the $2,000 mark. Resist the temptation to squander it as it builds. Get ready over the next six to 12 months to purchase land, adjacent to metropolitan areas, at distressed prices forced by the

34

business crunch. Use this time to build your knowledge of the procedures involved, while you build capital during the same period. If you have no family obligations strive for excellent purchases of vacant land. If you have obligations, concentrate on a triplex or fourplex, also buying adjacent land if possible. If you buy a triplex or fourplex, it is best to seek one on a lot that has room for additional units. It is quite possible you may be able to sell off adjacent land five years from now at a price sufficient to pay the mortgage on your building. Don't be discouraged if you run into "roadblocks" or brokers who tell you wild stories. Try to work with successful brokers who have made money themselves. You are only going to have one shot to fire in your real estate investment rifle, so make sure you hit the bulls -eye the first time.

Chapter 4

MAKE A PLAN

Many people often say "I am a wage earner. I have limited capital, most of which is used for family support. How can I buy real estate?"

The solution is in buying income-producing property. Vacant housing that can be bought very cheaply and rerented quickly is a sound candidate, especially residential housing in a suburban neighborhood on a busy street that will go commercial. It is not necessary for the rental payment to cover the entire cost of the mortgage, plus taxes. If it covers 80% of the cost, that is sufficient. You are not in there to make money as a landlord. That is of secondary importance. If you keep the property more than two years, you will have the opportunity to raise rents on whatever tenant occupies it anyway.

The important thing, as a wage-earner, is to find a situation where you can free your salary for opportunities that may arise. If you are speculating, it isn't even necessary that you stick to apartments. In fact, to solve the wage-earner's dilemma it is probably better to avoid apartments and turn your attention instead to residential housing going commercial, to producing farms with highway frontage, or other income-producing property.

When you tell a broker you are interested in property that generates income sufficient to cover most of the mortgage payment, the broker's brain immediately cranks out apartments - a fixed response. Your business opportunity probably lies in other types of income-producing properties, and there are many. Growing marketable timber on property with highway frontage is just one, suburban crop-bearing orchards are another. Producing farm land with either highway frontage or encroaching suburban housing is another; 50-50 share-cropping can be arranged. Use your imagination. While the fact that one is a wage-earner may seem an insurmountable obstacle to most of the general public, you should not see it as an obstacle but as an opportunity! Anything that discourages the general public from grabbing up the opportunities just leaves that money from lucrative situations for your benefit. The general public is interested only in well-known opportunities where risks are high and rewards are low. If you seek to make money in chunks you have to go into lesser-known fields, lesser-known areas where there are SURMOUNTABLE obstacles that discourage the general public.

THE WAGE EARNER'S LAMENT

When presented with these ideas, many say: "I realize this is sound advice, but I don't have time; I work 40 to 50 hours a week and there is no time left to search out these opportunities." You can gain 40 hours per month! Do you really want to make some money in real estate? It takes an average of 100 to 120 hours of actual negotiating and inspecting time to handle each deal. If you can make $5,000 per deal (a very conservative figure), that works out to $50 per hour.

There are two main sources of getting more time to search out profitable real estate speculations. The first source is to use 10 to 25 hours per week of your helpmate's time. She can check out deals, check ads, make phone calls, set up appointments for weekends, make initial broker contacts, eliminate many properties by visual inspection, and set up three to five of the best deals for your inspection on a Saturday. These things are a tremendous help, including such mundane tasks as obtaining and marking local maps, and by reading books on real estate. Chances are she will have much more fun with this kind of activity than spending most of her day hassling with three-foot-high people.

Another tremendous source of what we call "opportunity time" is also available, if you are really serious about making some real estate money. To gain 20 hours per month, just pull the plug of your television set out of the wall. If you negotiate one good deal, that small act can make thousands of dollars for you. The plug can be easily reattached after you have negotiated your first profitable purchase. By that time, however, you may just want to leave it unplugged. If you are trying this for the first time, note it isn't enough to pull the plug out of the wall - for best results, clip it off. For those who lament the loudest about "no time," the experience of "pulling the plug" can be similar to a heavy smoker going "cold turkey."

Perhaps you don't believe that the "gray lantern" steals your time. Let's face it, though. If you have no speculative capital, no definite plan with a time limit for accumulating some, and no time to work on either the plan or the acquisition, SOMETHING is stealing your time, embezzling your future! It takes a minimum of 100 hours to negotiate a profitable deal. On your first deal, it may take 200 hours because part of your time will be spent in the learning process, using less familiar methods. These time estimates do not include driving time. If you expect to "just happen on to" a grand opportunity in two to four hours of effort, forget it. It just doesn't work that way most of the time. Yet many folks expect the deal to pop that fast and give up easily if it doesn't.

If one wishes to avoid turmoil, chaos, and confusion, it is necessary to have a plan. Even a bad plan is better than no plan. Only by having a definite plan will you avoid being tossed about haphazardly by the winds of fate. Only with a plan will you be able to

make intelligent decisions, rational moves, and avoid
emotional ill-timed crowd behavior. There are great
changes that will take place in the U.S.A. and in the
world before 1980 rolls around. The better you plan,
the more you will benefit - even if your plan has to be
changed several times along the way.

What IS unusual is to seek definitely to project
wide-scale change a decade into the future. Most folks
are not used to doing so. Economists have special
statistical tools, some widely used and some quite
secret, which they try to use to project future economic activity. It is not an easy thing to project and
this discourages the average individual, particularly
if he has no tested, practiced, precise methods at
hand upon which to rely.

Not only are projections far into the future difficult - the results themselves are hard to accept,
especially if such results do not agree with prevailing
crowd opinion. If you make a professional projection
and obtain a result that is opposite to prevailing opinion, opposite to what governments and other special-
interest groups are preaching, you, too, may find
such conclusions difficult to accept. Yet, they are an
essential part of any good plan. Suppose, for example, you had walked down Fifth Avenue in New York
during the 1930's and told an acquaintance that within
three decades, California would be the most populous
state in the Union. Not only would your companion
look at you with astonishment - the idea of calling the
"men in the white coats" would have occurred. Such
a projection undertaken at a time when there were
still corduroy roads being used across the California
desert, would have been a very good one; in fact,
such a projection would have made a multimillionaire
out of anyone who was willing to back that projection
with a few hundred dollars or a few thousand dollars
of well-selected real estate commitments. The point
is, just because a projection is not widely accepted

by prevailing crowd opinion, does not mean the projection is inaccurate or invalid.

HOW MUCH CAPITAL DO YOU NEED?

About $1,500 is the practical minimum to begin speculating in real estate. You can start with less, but the really good deals don't start appearing until you can cough up at least $1,500 down. The average Joe, looking for a house or piece of property is hard-pressed to come up with over a thousand dollars - so he disappears from the scene as a competitive bidder once you pass the $1,500 level. Of course, if you have over $1,500 capital to spec with you can start making chunks of money that much faster.

The next step is to educate yourself in the field. A good start is by reading William Nickerson's books, "How I Turned $1000 into $3 Million in Real Estate in My Spare Time" and "How to Make a Fortune Today Starting From Scratch." Every library and book-store of any size have these two books. Grab them and read them. It is surprising how many real estate brokers have never read this millionaire's writings. Mr. Nickerson was a wage slave so long that even after he had made his first several hundred thousand dollars, he couldn't bear to leave the 9 to 5 job with the Telephone Company! If you think you are starting from a rugged situation, let him tell you about how he started, and you will find out you have many advantages.

The second person whom you wish to visit is a man named George Bockl, who wrote "How to Use Leverage to Make Money in Local Real Estate." Mr. Bockl is an inspiration on commercial property and improved property, precisely the kind that stands to gain most in value today. Let him show you how to spec improved property.

Make up your mind right now that you will pursue a course of self-education in the field and read anything you can get your hands on. So much the better if you live near a university that offers formal training. This educational process must be begun promptly for it is time-consuming and will require some weeks before you feel sure and confident.

Your next step, after reading the recommended material, is to get your eyes opened in your own area. You want to wheel and deal within 45 minutes driving time (maximum distance) from where you now live. You want to buy wholesale, not retail. You want to spec improved property, not bare land.

After reading all this information, you will no longer be putty in the hands of a broker. You'll know where and how to buy real estate wholesale yourself or how to get your broker to produce the best "need to sell" situations for you so you can buy well below current market. Set your goals. Lay them out. Type them out on a sheet of paper. Take a detailed map of the areas in which you are interested and draw boundaries to the areas you are going to explore. Stick to them. Don't deviate.

This information should be presented to the brokers with whom you hope to work and build rapport. How can he help you make a bundle if he doesn't know your specific goals, boundaries, objectives? If you have to reject eight out of the first 10 brokers you contact, so be it: don't be surprised if you have to reject 18 out of the first 20 you contact. It only takes one good broker to bring you that super-hot deal.

The first thing you need is a HUNGRY broker in the area you have selected. A fact of life is that most brokers are not "hungry"; poor perhaps, but not hungry for action. How do you locate a "hungry" broker? Very simple. You walk into his place of business and quickly ask, "What do you have that I can make $10,000 to $20,000 on? That's what I'm looking for." In nine cases out of 10, a strange look will pass across his face, then a sickly laugh will follow, with the words, "Isn't everybody?" That is how you can tell a non-hungry broker. Only in rare cases will the strange look, the sickly laugh and comment be missing. A broker who is hungry for action will jump out of his chair and try to find out if you are serious and then, believe it or not, try to help you make that money.

Now you can easily tell the difference. You will find it much easier to work through a broker than on your own. Hungry brokers, particularly, will go the extra mile in breaking deadlocked negotiations between buyers, sellers, and lenders. Knowing one or more hungry brokers who are active and energetic in the areas you have selected is a definite advantage.

It is also a shortcut. Everybody is used to dealing with the retailers of property. They do not know where to FIND the wholesalers. The retailers of property are the tract-house pushers, boondocks land salesmen, small brokers, very large brokers, subsequent owners, etc. These are the people the general public is used to dealing with.

The wholesalers are estate trustees, banks carrying bad paper, probates, attorneys, original farm owners, the sheriff. You deal with a wholesaler because you want to buy cheap or not at all. How are you going to buy and make a substantial profit if you pay built-in retail margins on real estate? You should be talking to the owner of the property or to the guy who owns the real estate firm, not one of his hirelings. The hireling's job is to move the goods at full ticket. He is not going to be able to wheel and deal with you where his boss might.

If you don't know any bankers, any attorneys, any original farm owners, any folks who act as trustees for estates, it is time you got to know some. Cultivate such relationships. They will be most valuable to you in the future. Let these people know you are looking for good property, priced for quick sale - substantially below market.

By employing these techniques you can make a year's income. Therefore, if the techniques take time, rest assured that the final reward can be worth it. The reading in the field is tough and some of it boring. Broker indifference is widespread, and lenders blow hot and cold. You must send out feelers to appropriate sources of potential purchases and train yourself to personally check every available source.

For those folks who are willing and able to surmount these obstacles, purchases carefully engineered at below conservative appraisals can lead to huge capital gains. You will have to go the extra mile and initiate a substantial amount of the effort yourself; this is in contrast to the general public. They always seem to take the path of least resistance. The first obstacle they encounter deters them, so competition will be limited and the field is wide open. If, however, you are easily swayed, you will be putty in the hands of the broker. It is up to you to decide which path you wish to take.

Chapter 5

THE WRONG WAY TO BUY A HOUSE
TO LIVE IN - THE RIGHT WAY

Sooner or later, almost every family has, as its
goal, the ownership of a nice home of their very own.
Unfortunately, according to your author's guidelines,
over 90% of these families will buy that home in the
wrong way. Very few will buy it according to money-
making principles, and that's good news for you; it
means you will have little competition!

The wrong way for the young family to buy a
house is to go out and buy a brand new tract house at
full ticket retail, or around there. That's the most
expensive, least money-making way to do things!
Not only do you pay full ticket, but you get bare landscaping, bare interior, the new house "bugs," pay
substantial salesman's commission and advertising
costs (oh, we know it's not spelled out in the price
that way, but buyer pays these costs nevertheless),
and all sorts of other expenses. This goes for town-
houses, new houses, tract houses and other related
real estate. Further, if you buy one of these new
tract houses and have to sell before the tract is fin-
ished, you may have to sell at a loss because you will
be competing with the developer who is also trying to
sell houses. You may have to sell at a price below
what you paid the developer, to entice the new buyer.
If a broker handles the transaction for you, you could
lose additional amounts, thousands of dollars in commissions just to pay broker's fee. New houses look
nice, the houses are usually beautifully decorated pro-
fessionally, the salesmen are well-dressed, charming,
and persuasive - but you support the whole shebang.
No bargains here!

There are many right ways to buy a house to live in, but you first should have some ground rules or principles so that you know when to deal, how to deal, and where to deal. The first, and probably most important principle is this, IF YOU CAN'T MAKE A MINIMUM OF $5,000 - $15,000 (SET YOUR OWN FIGURE), ON ANY DEAL IN A REASONABLE TIME, DON'T BUY IT. Buying a house to live in does not mean that you have to avoid making money: Just because you need a place to live, doesn't mean that you should take a loss, or avoid making money. Why be penalized financially just because you are going to live there?!

Yes, I recognize you may have a difficult time convincing your spouse that the way most couples buy houses is totally wrong, and this way is right. But your perseverance will pay off. However much money you are making, there is no reason why you can't satisfy both your desires at the same time, namely, buying a house to live in, and making one year's income or more on the transaction, if you should have to turn around and sell it.

The fact that you plan to live in a house should not change the way you buy it! Since, for most families, a house purchase (to live in) will be the biggest purchase they make, it should be done intelligently, and profitably, or avoided unless it can be done in that manner. Again, if you can't make a minimum of at least $5,000 on any real estate deal, don't buy it. Go in with the idea of making money; think positive! Search out the profitable deal, even though you plan to occupy the house for a time. In California, the average family occupies their own home for approximately 4.8 years before they move. Therefore, if the chances are excellent that you will be moving within five years, why not buy to make a profit in the first place!? Whether you live there or not?! Do it right the first time.

It is important that you have a plan if you are seeking to purchase a house to live in. That plan should make you money as one of its goals. Purchase only where you find a "need-to-sell" situation at a price where you can make money.

What about duplexes, or triplexes? These are great for families starting out who need a place to live, a good speculation, and an income to help them with the mortgage. Nevertheless, don't purchase them unless you find them for sale below market, at a price where you can turn around and make a profit. In general, the definite possibility of wage/price/rent controls make the outlook for income property dim. Last time, "four or less" income units were exempt, which meant duplexes and triplexes were in the clear. But, on properties involving five or more income units, I predict that you will be strapped in by rent controls once again in the future. Rent controls are not gone forever, by a long shot.

Should you build on a lot you own? No, definitely not! Again, this is the wrong way to get a house to live in. The only time you might build is where you can build at a cost way below market. That is, either by being in the business, being in the building trades, doing the bulk of the work yourself, including usage of moonlighting workmen. It doesn't usually make sense to build when you can pick up below-market properties with a little effort. Why pay full ticket construction costs when you can buy already-built properties for less than it costs you to build?

A debt moratorium (a suspension of property payments without allowing lender to foreclose) such as in the last depression, could become a very important piece of legislation.

Even with recession approaching, your author is not too worried about well-structured, usable, rentable real estate purchased well below market at the present time. Why? Because a fluctuating currency unit, with additional printing press money, with expanded credit, is expected as one of the frequent government attempts to <u>cure</u> the recession. Pay back in paper currency units of less purchasing power. "Money pollution" was a term invented by the FORECASTER newsletter and your author, who first coined the phrase. It is now used as an apt description of current events by many notables. The debtor gains, the lender loses, in a money pollution situation. Mortgage holders are note holders, just as any other lender.

<u>Summary</u>: Buy a house to make money, not to spend it, whether you plan to live in it or not!

Chapter 6

HOW SHOULD YOU BUY?

There are two ways to go through life. When we are younger and have no capital, we have to market our services to build capital. When we grow older and a little smarter, we shoot for big capital gains and try to make the capital do the work. In other words, the goal is to "do your thing" while the dollars go to work for you.

In real estate it is often possible to make one to three years' income on a single good investment with limited risk. Good, buildable real estate, purchased right, can bail you out even if you make a little mistake in the purchase. If you purchase land in the path of growth, your purchases will be mostly unwelcome and uninvited by the establishment. Large companies or political bodies that have plans for developing certain areas do not particularly want you to purchase that pre-development land. Why? If you help tie up the supply, they will have to pay you fierce prices for it in years to come, and you can hold it for ransom. They will not be in favor of your purchasing such land for speculation - for they may have to buy it back in 5 or 10 years for a much higher price.

Since you probably have little capital to work with, it is recommended that you buy it on time, writing the interest charges off your income taxes. The skilled breadwinner easily earns five figures, particularly with Saturdays and overtime. In many families, there are two workers, skilled or unskilled. In both cases, they find themselves in a minimum 30%-40% tax bracket. Professionals, such as doctors and attorneys, find themselves in much higher brackets.

Since Uncle Sam is going to share your profits, what you have to do is structure your real estate purchase in such a way that he will help you to carry the purchase. If a person puts 5% down on an acreage parcel, and pays interest only for five years, he can deduct that interest from his income tax each year as he pays it. If he is in a 30% to 50% bracket (as most people are), Uncle Sam will be picking up one-third to one-half of the cost. Although the taxes on vacant property are not very high, he can also deduct the property taxes from his income tax.

In general, it doesn't pay to make commitments in any one investment of less than $1,500. Those with restricted funds should try to accumulate capital until they can manage $1,500 chunks. If you make a $1,500 commitment in a certain category and the category doubles in value, you have something worthwhile.

The "$20 to $50-per-month" attitude is one of the false illusions sponsored by the Debtor's Society. If you do not have the willpower to accumulate these $20 to $50-a-month amounts until you have $1,500, it is hard to see how you will have the willpower to be a financial individual when you do have some investment success. If you are out of practice at accumulating small amounts of capital and changing them into larger quarterly or annual chunks of capital, it is respectfully suggested that you practice accumulation rather than plunging $20 to $50 amounts into commitments that are spread far too thin.

For example, far too much boondocks overpriced real estate is peddled simply because it can be bought for "no money down and $20 per month". As you move from the "$100 down" style real estate to the "$1,500 down" style real estate, you may discover at least 10 times more profitable opportunities to consider in the higher down-payment real estate situation. When making purchases of distressed real estate at 40% below appraised value, it is almost always necessary to have at least $1,500 down-payment minimum.

And, of course, you have read in the past how banks and savings and loans pay higher interest returns to the larger accounts. It is fully realized that a student has just as hard a time accumulating $20 per month for investment, as a professional man accumulating $1,000 per month. No one is belittling anyone's efforts to put aside $20 or $50 a month for investment; it is merely being pointed out that one can invest more safely and more profitably if those $20 or $50-per-month amounts are held out of investments until several hundred dollars have accumulated.

There is no need to start out with big parcels, but you should buy a piece big enough so that you can carve it up later, a minimum parcel purchase of three to five acres. There are a lot of more mature folks reading this book right now who probably wished someone had pushed them into real estate when they were in their 20's or 30's. They could be $100,000 or $200,000 richer by now. If you buy real estate on the fringes of great metropolitan areas in your 20's or early 30's, you will have the option of continuing to work or not in 10 to 15 years. It will not be necessary for you to work 40 to 45 years for some anonymous corporation for a pension.

There are many folks around who say, "Gee, I just can't afford any real estate right now - particularly several acres." Hogwash! Anybody who can buy a $6,000 car, or make car payments of $150 to $250 a month, can buy $20,000 to $35,000 worth of real estate. Usual terms may involve payment of as little as one half of one percent of the principal amount per month.

BUY FOR PAPER

When purchasing such acreage you should try to get a low down payment; $500 to $1,500 is an adequate

amount to risk.   If you shop around, you will discover that while interest rates on houses have risen
as high as 9%, interest rates on vacant land are quite
often 6%, 7% and 8%.   In other words, you may be
able to carry that land at 3% less interest than a con-
ventional house mortgage.   Furthermore, you can
often talk the seller into taking back from 75% to
90% of the amount borrowed.

If you are working with a progressive broker, you
can tell the broker that you want to pay interest only
for the first five years, with principal payments to
start only in the sixth year, as previously outlined.
A broker who is actively seeking commissions will
sincerely try to help you find property that meets
your particular structural requirements.   If you buy
land from companies, you will discover their interest rates are normally 8%, 9%, and so on.   But if
you deal with businessmen or farmers who want to
retire, you may find lots of them who will give you a
6% interest rate.

If you are the buyer, it is up to you to call the
shots and insist on the price and terms you want.   For
professional people whose tax bracket is over 25%, it
is recommended that you buy this land ONLY if it
meets the specific conditions outlined as to price and
utility.   To get proper leverage you should pay a
MAXIMUM OF 20% CASH DOWN, preferably no more
than 10% down.   As a high-bracket earner, you want
to write the interest charges off your income tax.
DO NOT pay an interest rate of over 9%.   It will look
highly embarrassing a few years from now if interest
rates go down sharply.   If you pay 10% down, make
sure you get terms of five to ten years or more to
pay the balance.

In light of what we know about the coming recession, it is going to take an excellent piece of real
estate to buck the trend.   At worst, if you buy for
90% paper and the price falls, you can always write

off your 10% down payment and let the property go back to the seller.

Now, if you lose your down payment - and you are a solvent debtor - you can turn right around and buy three or four pieces of similar property at the new LOWER price! The loss of a down payment should not trouble you at all. The purchasing power of your other cash-form assets would increase sharply. The purchasing power of your savings would go up sharply, as well as your other liquid investments. Instead of three acres, you might wind up with 20 for the same money.

We do not envision such a transaction happening - when wisely selected - but it is good to be able to have the particular assurance that you can let the seller foreclose and take it over with little loss.

Example: Suppose you buy a small, flat, buildable, usable parcel with utilities, near the city limits, say five acres at $2,000 per acre. Five years go by and you are now ready to sell that property for $20,000 to $25,000. You call your friendly broker and he says, "Sure, we can get that for you. Shall we set it up?" You give him the okay and a month or so later you get another call saying, "Fine, we have the deal ready to go through with $2,500 down and $25,000 for the parcel. Then you say, "Hey, wait a minute. Salesmen's commissions and selling costs are going to eat up most of the entire cash down payment. I want at least half down." Then the broker will say, "Sorry, nothing doing; can't get it for you."

In other words, if you are going to have to sell for mostly paper (first trust deeds or first mortgages), you must buy it the same way. Don't spend more on the down payment than you can afford to gamble and lose. You should have a special clause in the sales contract that limits your risk to the property alone. For $25 or so, your attorney will write up such a clause and plug it in the contract for you.

Many standard sales contracts already carry this provision. For example, if you buy a $10,000 property with $1,000 down, and later forfeit, you don't want the guy coming after you for $9,000. Your attorney can insert a specific clause in the sales contract that limits your risk to the $1,000 down payment plus any subsequent payments.

MORTGAGE RATES. INTEREST RATES. SHOULD YOU BUY IN THESE DAYS OF HIGH MORTGAGE COSTS?

Interest rates can only perform three ways over the coming year. Either they will (a) go up, (b) go down, or (c) stay about the same. If they are going to (a) go up, by all means, you should be buying now - you'll be a hero later. If they are going to (b) go down, you can always refinance at lower rates later, so you should be looking and buying now. If interest rates (c) stay the same, and you have other good reasons for buying now, the question is immaterial. Score: 2 reasons for buying now, and 1 neutral.

Those folks who bought houses when mortgage rates were 10%-11% are hereby advised to get them refinanced at today's lower rates. Mortgage money is now available at annual rates of $9\frac{1}{4}$% to $9\frac{1}{2}$%, and sometimes even less, depending on how badly the savings and loans want to write mortgages. Don't sit with those expensive mortgages. Pay them off! The savings are TREMENDOUS. Perhaps you have a $30,000 30-year mortgage at $10\frac{1}{2}$%. Saving 1% of the interest cost the first year (by refinancing at a rate 1% lower), your first year's saving would be $300. Now, compound that $300 over the 30-year life of the mortgage (during which you will have the use of that saved money). Let us say you save $290 the second year. Now, compound that $290 interest saving over the remaining 29 years of the mortgage, say at the 5 3/4% rate of interest now paid by savings and loans. You have calculated so far only the savings of two years on that 30-year mortgage. Can you imagine what those savings would amount to by time you calculated and compounded the savings over the entire life of the mortgage?

Maybe you do have a $600 early payoff penalty. You are still far, far better off to pay that penalty and renegotiate your mortgage at a much lower rate. The savings can easily amount to many thousands of dollars for those of you with a high-rate mortgage. Kick that interest rate downward! Even if you keep that house only five or ten years, you will still be better off to pay the penalty for early payoff and seize advantage of today's lowered mortgage rate.

Make a try to get a transferable clause inserted as part of the early payoff in the mortgage. You want to get that mortgage renegotiated, not only at a lower interest rate, but renegotiated so that you can transfer it at that same new lowered interest rate to any new buyer, no matter what interest rates are in the future. It is still worthwhile to pay off a high-interest mortgage if you can get a significant drop in the interest rate on a new mortgage, even if you cannot get a "transferable to any new buyer at $9\frac{1}{4}\%$" clause inserted in your new mortgage. But try to get the clause inserted. It is important and will make it easier to resell your property if mortgage rates at some time in the future rise to 12%.

A lower interest transferable loan on your property, that goes with the property, could possibly make your holding worth several thousand dollars more. Don't overlook this possibility for engineering a future capital gain. The lender will probably scream when you try to get a transferable clause inserted, but make the try anyway. The lender will tell you it is seldom done and seldom asked for. True, but that should not prevent you from asking for it. Even if your chances of getting it inserted

are only one in ten, it is worth the old college try.
Don't be afraid to shop six to ten lenders for interest
rates and let them know in all honesty that you are
seeking the best rate and best deal.   Competition has
flooded some of the savings and loans with money
right now and the time is right for you to ask them
for a highly competitive loan.

POINTS.   HOW TO BEAT THE COST

Some lending institutions now charge one point or
more (1% of the total), as an additional financing
charge, but many lenders don't charge points (banks,
insurance companies).   So, avoid lenders who charge
points if you don't want to pay points, and go where
they don't charge points.   Simple.   The lender who
doesn't charge points, may charge you 1/8% or $\frac{1}{4}$%
more interest, but if you refinance later, that's immaterial, too, isn't it?   And what's one point where
you have a chance to make or save $10,000, $20,000,
$50,000, $100,000? It's really immaterial, isn't it?
Nit picking.   Make the chunk of money, first!   Save
the chunk of money on the next house you buy for your
family!

PREPAYMENT PENALTIES

If you borrow on a mortgage and later refinance
at lower rate, original lender may ask for a penalty
payment called a PREPAYMENT PENALTY.   On a
$30,000 mortgage a typical penalty might be $600.
There are THREE ways to beat the prepayment penalty.
First, if you are borrowing, to buy property,
READ that mortgage contract carefully first, and
STRIKE OUT any clause that calls for a PREPAYMENT
PENALTY.   SHOP YOUR MORTGAGE!   Get a copy of
the contract in advance.   Some lenders don't like to
give you a copy to read in advance, but that's tough.
Folks recently took reluctant lenders to court and won
their case.   BEST WAY TO BEAT prepayment PEN-

ALTY is NOT to SIGN for mortgage that carries one in the first place. Preventive medicine!

Second way to beat prepayment penalty is to look for ACCELERATED PAYMENT clause. Example: we recently purchased a building and didn't like the loan on it even though it was necessary for the sake of the deal to go through with it. After owning the building a few months, we decided to get rid of existing mortgage. However, mortgage contract had clause with stiff prepayment penalty. We found ANOTHER clause, however, which said that borrower could pay UP TO 20% of the original amount of the mortgage in ANY given MONTH. In order to get rid of the mortgage and arrange new financing, we made FIVE separate PAYMENTS 20% of mortgage each month and in five months had paid up entire mortgage WITHOUT PENALTY of any kind. Lender was surprised, but had no choice! The second way to beat prepayment penalties - search for accelerated payment clauses that allow you to make larger payments in any one month. Use them to pay off mortgage. Creative financing!

Third, to beat prepayment penalties, refinance only when there is interest differential of 1% or more. (Example: paying up a $9\frac{1}{2}\%$ mortgage to go to $8\frac{1}{2}\%$ new financing.) That way prepayment penalty is INSIGNIFICANT in relation to INTEREST SAVINGS. Another way to beat prepayment penalty is to get new buyer to assume existing loan.

In summary, there are several ways to avoid prepayment penalties from costing you money, both before and after signing the mortgage. Worrying about prepayment penalties is therefore immaterial, and useless, and should not discourage you from buying or financing foreclosures!

Chapter 7

USE ESCROWS FOR PROFIT

As more and more real estate investors begin speculating in land and building, most first-time investors encounter a confusing word called "escrow". Escrow is just a fancy name for a third party holding the bet once a deal has been agreed upon. With a fancy name, higher fees can be charged.

One prime way to use escrows for profits in buying is always try to get the seller to pay all escrow expenses! A broker or a sharp seller sometimes talks the poor buyer into paying 100% escrow expenses. Don't let them "snow" you. It is often customary for the seller to pay half of the escrow fee and the buyer to pay half. Never pay more than 50%. If you have an anxious seller, you can often talk him into paying the whole thing.

Normally, the escrow company has an attorney that will help you on small matters without charging. Consult him before you go into escrow if you have details that need ironing out. It is to your advantage to select the escrow company, if at all possible. It is preferable to deal with larger firms. If the seller is talked into paying all escrow expenses, however, you may have to go along with his selection of the company.

HOW TO GET LOWEST CHARGES ON ESCROWS, TITLE INSURANCE, AND CLOSING COSTS WHEN YOU BUY OR SELL PROPERTY

Most property buyers are not aware how much closing costs can run. Usually, when they buy their first house they are shocked to discover closing costs far in excess of what they anticipated. How do you beat the game? Let's go "inside the trade" for a peek.

Were you aware that many Escrow Companies and Title Companies sometimes have a tendency to charge "what the traffic will bear"? Yes, it is true that Title Companies and Escrow Companies charge different rates to different people. For example, Mr. Average Homebuyer may be charged a higher rate than others. A broker in the business may be charged a lower rate. The lowest is often charged to banks and savings and loan companies who deal in large numbers of properties and provide lots of business. How do you win the game? Simple. Whenever you are dealing with a Title Company, or Real Estate firm, specify that you want to be charged lowest bank rates on closing costs & title costs. Let them know that you are aware of the varying rate structure. Tell them that you want the lowest possible rate. Insist on it!

A LONG ESCROW

Best place to use a long escrow in land or building speculation is when you anticipate holding the property for a long time before the market rises (example, three to five years and up). Suppose you are buying a property for $25,000 which you hope to resell within five years for $45,000. You intend to pay $5,000 down and the remaining $20,000 at 6% interest over an extended period of time. Taxes are $600 per year. Interest for one year at 6%, on $20,000, is $1,200, or $100 per month. Taxes at $600 per year work out to $50 a month.

In other words, each month that you have the property tied up in escrow but don't legally own it, you save $100 on interest and $50 on taxes. That's $150 per month saving on each month of a long escrow. If you go into a 10-month escrow, you take the property off the market for 10 months and save 10 times $150, or $1,500. That's easy money, so use this little technique.

Long escrows are also preferable where you suspect the seller may not have told you all the facts pertaining to the property. A long escrow will make the "serpents" in the deal visible.

Long escrows are also handy where assessments are in progress. If the city is installing sewers, sidewalks, streetlights, etc., you may force the existing owner to pay those charges by tying it up in a long escrow - for your lesser expense and greater profit.

A SHORT ESCROW

You should use a short escrow under the following situations: (a) where ownership of the property will make you money or save you lots of money (example - you are shelling out $300 per month rent for an apartment where you could be living on the newly purchased property and pocketing the rent - sometimes a seller will permit you to occupy a property while it is tied up in escrow - so don't overlook this possibility); (b) where the net income per month from the purchase is large and you want to start collecting the funds quickly (example, if the $25,000 property yielded $800 per month income); (c) where there is a possibility for quick resale at a huge profit (example, you know about the new shopping center that will be built across the street in 180 days and you want that property quickly recorded so you can resell profitably).

HOW TO BEAT THE TAX ASSESSOR AND GET LOWER TAXES

Taxes are one of the big problems these days with property. There is a quick and easy way to get lower tax bills on distressed property, but few people do it. How is this little trick performed?

First, you must get a copy of the previous owner's tax bill. Second, figure out what the tax assessor thinks that property is worth at retail. Let's say, for example, you just purchased a property appraised at $90,000 for $65,000. When you look over the tax bill you might discover the assessor thinks the property is worth $90,000, and has assessed it accordingly.

But you only paid $65,000! Therefore, what you must do is to call the assessor and "request a re-assessment". You will have to provide him with papers proving that you only paid $65,000 for a property he has assessed much higher. He will probably re-assess that property at $65,000 to $70,000 the next year. This could save you $500 to $1,000 on your next year's taxes. If it is an income property, lower taxes mean less expense. Less expense means higher profits, more income. More income means you can sell that property for a higher price and bigger profits on the sale. Therefore, bothering the tax assessor is worthwhile, not only to save $500 to $1,000 per year on your taxes - but also to beef up your income statements so you can sell the property for a bigger price.

Requesting a re-assessment is also profitable in another way. If the trend in the neighborhood is to raise taxes every way, this might also cause the tax assessor to break that trend. It may discourage him from automatically assessing your property higher every year and boosting your tax bill. The author has used this strategy not once, but several times. It works! It's easy money! Do it, and put the extra cash in your pocket! In distressed property, it is necessary and vital to maximize profit by legally lowering property taxes when and where you can.

HOW TO SAVE ON REAL ESTATE COMMISSIONS

There is no law fixing real estate commissions. Firms may charge $\frac{1}{2}$% to 10%. Personally, your author has never paid over 5% when selling a property. California brokers may ask you for 6% - but you don't have to pay it. If they really want your listing, and it is a resalable property, you can offer them 3% to 5%. That 6% isn't "iron-clad" - even though the hustling broker may make it sound that way. <u>Negotiate</u> the commission. This little idea alone can save you several hundreds to many thousands of dollars.

Chapter 8

INFLATION HEDGING

Governments print money without backing. They expand credit through bookkeeping. Fiat money, printing-press money, over-expansion of credit, government overspending, all fuel the fires of inflation. Wage-price controls merely suppress evidence of this "behind-the-scenes" inflating. Those, such as yourself, who seek protection against "money pollution" can turn to inflation hedging.

There are four basic methods of inflation hedging you can use to protect yourself against sustained inflation and loss of purchasing power (rising prices).

When we speak of hedging or currency theory, these theories apply to any weak currency, not necessarily the dollar. A Frenchman might find a study of such theory just as valuable as an Englishman or an American or a Brazilian.

In inflation hedging you must know WHY the currency is weak. Knowing why will determine which four basic approaches to use to HEDGE the currency. When sustained inflation and weakened currencies go together and appear that they are going to be companions for the mid-term or long-term future, buying debt instruments such as mortgages is not a good method of profiting from them.

The FIRST way to hedge currency is to buy cash in the hopes of using it to buy goods at a discount later. In other words, you hoard lots of cash (some Americans do this with T-Bills currently, which pay about 6% interest - in hopes of employing that cash later to buy goods at 50¢ or 60¢ on the dollar). This method is not very satisfactory when a weakening currency is occurring at the same time as a sustained domestic inflation. Distinguish between a currency that is weak because of other circumstances (examples - war, natural catastrophe, poor crops, etc.) without sustained inflation, as opposed to a currency that is weak because of sustained inflation.

The SECOND basic approach to hedging inflation is a short-term one. This is actually selling rapidly-weakening currencies. This method is usually used when the currency is weak, sick and dropping fast, when you have to protect your assets denominated in that currency quick. A strong currency is purchased and a weak currency is simultaneously sold. This can be done through a London bank, Swiss bank, or a large sophisticated U.S. bank. It can usually only be done if you are an established businessman who has been doing business with the bank for many years. Though dealings with international banks are perfectly legal, they are presently being frowned upon.

A disadvantage with this method for the individual is that your local banker may not know how to do it for you. If you ask him to sell the pound sterling and buy the Swiss franc, he may give you a look as though you were one of the little green men from Mars who just walked into his office.

A second disadvantage of this method is that it is relatively costly over the short term. This is an expensive way to hedge, especially over a period of several years. It is only a valuable method when the currency is on the verge of being devalued in the near future. (For example, in the 1967 British devaluation this method made sense.)

The THIRD basic approach is to buy specie (gold coin, silver coin) and borrow. Borrow face value on the specie in the weak currency. For example, if you wanted to hedge the dollar you might buy a $1,000 bag of 40% silver half-dollar coins for $1,200, and borrow the $1,000 face-value unit by pledging it as collateral on a loan at the bank, at 9%. You would unofficially

have a hedge against dollar devaluation and the banker
would have a nice safe loan.   This method too is costly
in terms of interest charged, but it is more satisfactory for longer term hedges.   There is no currency
hedging method that IS NOT costly.

While this third approach is not an unusual approach to those people who regularly study coinage,
very few of the general public know about or use this
method.   Nor are many economists familiar with it.
It would work for any weak currency provided you
could get a loan denominated in that currency at a
reasonable rate.

Geographical considerations are sometimes a disadvantage.   If you had just two bags of specie you would
not want to go all the way to Israel or Egypt to pledge
those bags on a loan denominated in either the Israel
currency or Egyptian pound.

The FOURTH basic approach to hedging is perfectly satisfactory for long-term currency hedges.   It
is borrowing money in the suspect currency on highly
leveraged real estate purchased at a discount.   For
easy figuring, consider a property appraised at
$100,000.   You try to buy this property at a discount
in a feeble market for, say, $80,000.   Furthermore,
through tough negotiations you try to get $70,000 fi-
nancing on the $80,000 property.

You try to stack the deck in your favor in three
ways: (1) you denominate the loan in the weak currency, (2) you try to buy the real estate at a substantial discount from its normal market value so that
you can make a capital gain from the discounted price
when the market gets better, and (3) you let inflation
give you the hope to pay off the $70,000 with diluted
paper money during the same time period that the real
estate goes up in value on its own, and also goes up in
value because of a continued inflationary trend.

This fourth approach is probably the most satisfactory for a currency that is not too weak but continues

to get weaker at a very slow rate over a very long
time period. Few economists think of real estate
loans as a definite and specific method of hedging currency so it is not unusual that this method may never
be precisely outlined elsewhere.

This method has many advantages, in that loans
on real estate are almost always easy to get. It does
have disadvantages, however. It might be pretty hard
to get a loan in French francs, for instance, on a
$50,000 property located in the U.S. (if the French
franc was the currency you wanted to repay in). The
property employed in your hedging often has to be geo-
graphically located in an area conducive to loans in
the weakening currency. Another disadvantage is that
you have to learn a lot about specific properties and
real estate trading in general. You cannot employ this
method if you choose to remain uninformed regarding
methods of trading real estate. Surprisingly enough,
a substantial proportion of the population does choose
to remain voluntarily uninformed about real estate.

It is a good principle to always borrow as much
as possible when you purchase real estate for capital
gains. There are many reasons for this. One obvious
reason is that of limiting your risk to the smallest
possible down payment. There might be a garbage
dump or tannery going up nearby of which the seller
may not have informed you. Perhaps a depression
might strike suddenly without much warning, making
payments on property difficult. If you had 80% or 90%
financing you would have little to lose beyond your own
down payment; it forces the lender and seller to take
most of the risk.

Unless you have sufficient affluence it is best to
stick to properties that generate some sort of income
to help make payments. (Examples: producing farms,
residential and commercial rentals, etc.) Those with
six-figures net worth can afford to hedge non-income-
producing properties. Others might find cash payments
on non-income property burdensome.

The amazing thing is that those with the least net worth usually buy the over-priced, unimproved remote properties rather than the income-producers!

Another reason for borrowing as much as possible (when you hedge inflation through real estate) is to make eventual resale much easier. A $40,000 property with $30,000 in assumable transferable loans, is much easier to resell than a $40,000 property with a $15,000 nontransferable mortgage. Make the seller eat the paper or give you bigger discounts! A $40,000 property with a $15,000 first mortgage is often hard to refinance via the second-mortgage route. On the other hand, if the first mortgage is $30,000 to begin with and is transferable, you may get a second mortgage without difficulty for $5,000 additional. It makes resale so much easier. The interest rate on a first mortgage is almost always lower, much lower, than on a second mortgage. Therefore, the higher the first mortgage, the cheaper your interest payments will be.

BUYING BACK YOUR I. O. U. 'S

When hedging inflation through real estate you have already seen why it pays to get the seller to take back the second mortgage rather than giving him a huge chunk of cash. Here is a little-known secret of making additional profits: buy back your own second mortgage at a discount after the transaction is completed. Perhaps you buy a $40,000 property, assume a $20,000 first mortgage, paying $5,000 cash and forcing the seller to eat a second mortgage of $15,000 at 8%. By our previous rules, the property should appraise out conservatively at least $50,000 to meet our standards. Once the seller has accepted a $15,000 second mortgage from you as part of the purchase, there is nothing to prevent you from offering to buy that second mortgage from him at a discount! It may surprise the seller to get such an offer from you, but you will be amazed at how often you can repurchase your own I. O. U. at 70¢ to 90¢ on the dollar.

Suppose you borrowed a thousand dollars and you signed an interest-bearing I. O. U. Suppose one month later you offered $900 cash for that note for your own I. O. U. In any field <u>outside</u> real estate, the lender would not be happy to get that $900 cash offered for a thousand-dollar interest-bearing note. In real estate, however, chances are he would smile and grab the offer. It works. Not only do you try to buy the property at a substantial discount, you also try to get it financed in such a manner that you can buy back your own paper at a discount.

Many real estate loans have a non-assumable loan clause. They stick in a little phrase that says in effect, "if the property is resold before the loan is paid off, the entire amount of the loan becomes immediately due and payable." You must strike out such a clause when you are negotiating the deal. You must make these loans transferable to ANY NEW BUYER at a FIXED interest rate. That is part of the secret of negotiating a good real estate deal and one of the methods to use in hedging currencies through leveraging real estate. The lender will tell you it is seldom done.

For real estate capital gains in inflation hedging (a) finance as much as possible, (b) make those loans transferrable at a fixed interest rate, (c) seek to buy back your own second mortgages, first mortgages, or I. O. U.'s at a substantial discount under their face value, (d) buy the property only if it can be purchased at a substantial discount from conservative appraisals, (e) stick to income-generating properties unless your net worth permits you to make payments without burden, (f) unlike the general public, don't remain voluntarily unknowledgeable of real estate opportunities.

Chapter 9

INTEREST RATES --
TOO HIGH TO BUY OR SELL?

At this writing, the prime rate is fluctuating at around 7%. Why can't you get money at 7%? Simple. It's a privilege of the banking industry. You must pay far more at the bank.

In fact, in spite of widely publicized prime rates of 7%, there are few businessmen and individuals who are getting such low rates. Many "best risk" people and firms with fully collaterized loans are paying rates of 9% to 11% and more. Do you know anyone who is getting bank loans at 7%? While a substantial prime rate cut would probably be short-lived, and soon result in pressure on the U.S. dollar, a prime rate cut would receive the most widespread publicity imaginable. It would also foster new financing by firms, by individuals, and by government itself. They would be falling over each other to get to the market quickly to borrow money. The first step for success in playing the interest rate cycle is to review all your loans. Do you have a present mortgage at over 10%? If so, you probably should refinance. Mortgages are now available at 8 3/4% to 9 1/4% for individuals. Do you have a car loan at 12% to 14%? If so, perhaps you should borrow money on a house rather than on a car. Borrowing on a car and making payments is a very expensive way to borrow money.

If the prime rate is cut, you may be able to pressure your banker into a slightly lower mortgage rate on a house or building you want to buy, or to refinance one you already own.

Just consider what a 2% interest differential means on a 30 year mortgage. The savings could run into many thousands of dollars on a medium-priced home. In some cases perhaps as much as half the value of the home could be saved.

There are only three possibilities for interest rates. They will (a) either go up, (b) go down, or (c) stay the same. If (c) they stay the same, obviously there's no reason for you to worry about financing real estate at today's rates, providing you have the ability and income to make the payments.

If (a) they go up, today's interest rate is going to be pretty good, and look good to a new buyer, especially if you can transfer today's interest rate to him on a transferable loan. Therefore, it is to your advantage to borrow at today's rate to finance deals which (you have analyzed) can make you substantial profit.

What about the case where (b) interest rates go down? Simple -- you refinance. In fact, periods of high interest rates often make need-to-sell properties appear on the market, the kind of properties you want to buy cheaply and REMARKET. Some of your author's best deals have been made in a period when interest rates are high. After they go down, no need to be stuck with a high interest rate, just refinance the mortage or find a new lender and pay off the old one.

Many modern mortgages contain interest penalty clauses, where, if you pay off the mortgage early, to refinance at a lower rate, you get hit with the penalty.

On an average home, this penalty clause might cost $500-$600. Assuming your mortgage has this penalty clause, perhaps to the tune of $500, it would still be advantageous for you to pay the penalty if you can get a good break on your mortgage rate. What does $500 penalty mean when savings of many thousand dollars are at stake? It's a pittance.

Of course, there will be many who will not renegotiate their high-interest mortgages. They will

possibly be too slow, too uninformed, or too lazy
to do anything about the mortgage and its refinancing.
Perhaps their lending institution will give them a
"snow job" on their first approach, and they will be
too discouraged to press the issue (after all, what
lending institution wants to substitute a lower rate
mortgage for a higher interest mortgage?). Mortgage
renegotiation is not a practice generally engaged in
by the public, but for those who take the time and
trouble to do so, it can be of immense monetary
importance.

Another way to profit on a prime rate cut, or
a downturn in interest rates, is if you have non-
mortage loans outstanding. Why should you be paying 10%, 11%, 14%, 18% on department store charge
accounts, if the prime rate falls? Get those loans
renegotiated and don't be slow about it. Whether
those loans are unsecured, or fully secured, you
should get a lower loan rate if interest rates in
general go down. Sometimes lending institutions
are quite slow to point out these obvious facts to
their customers.

Hanging real estate deals can be profitably
negotiated after a prime rate cut. It has been suggested to use no more than 10% or 20% down payment
when buying real estate, forcing the seller to carry
the mortgage or loan paper at a low rate. This saves
you the trouble of negotiating with more sophisticated
lending institutions, and having to pay points. If you
have a $40,000 real estate deal hanging, with your
offer of 10% down and 90% on a 15-year loan, at 9%
interest, you could use a period of lower interest
rates to sweeten the deal in your favor. For example,
you might raise your down payment to 15%, but force
the reluctant seller to carry the mortgage at 7%
instead of 9%, perhaps extending the term of the
loan as well.

70

Lenders would have you believe that mortgage rates that they quote you are not negotiable. Don't you believe that for a minute. It's _negotiable_ from the word GO. While the particular lending officer may not have much to say about it, he probably sits on a loan committee that _does_ have the final say. Also, don't be afraid to use other business with the lending institution as a lever to get a more favorable rate. It has been done, is being done, and will be done in the future. The first rate quoted you is only a _starting_ point. Same way when you're dealing with private sellers. Here, too, it's all negotiation from the word GO. You have even wider room to move with a private owner or seller than with a lending institution.

All students of real estate speculation should recognize the leverage possibilities and lower carrying costs inherent in a cut in interest rates in general and in the prime rate in particular. However, you probably won't have much time to make your new offers and get the sellers' decisions, so you will have to act quickly. Push on your deals. Don't let it lie in some real estate broker's office for several months while the seller "hems and haws"! Put a 10-day or a 15-day time limit on any offers you make. Force the seller to make up his mind, either positively or negatively.

A word about counter offers. When you are buying or selling properties, or negotiating interest rates with a buyer or seller who is going to carry the paper, always make counter offers. If he offers 10% and you started out with 6%, offer 7%. If he comes back with 9%, go up to $7\frac{1}{2}$%. Never accept _his_ offer. Always make a counter offer. He accepts your offer, you don't accept his! If you're $5,000 apart, and you would buy the property at that price, nevertheless make a counter offer. After all, you can _always_ accept his offer if you feel like it. This tip alone may save you hundreds and thousands of dollars on your next real estate purchase or sale! It could pay for hundreds of copies of this book to give to your friends!

Chapter 10

INFLATION RATES

In projecting ahead for a full decade, you assume an annual inflation rate (loss of purchasing power) of 5% to 9% per year with only brief interruptions. When you have an inflation rate of 6% per year and you can borrow money at a prime rate of 6% per year, the money you borrow costs you nothing. In fact, if the interest is tax deductible, you actually gain. The secret, of course, is to borrow that money and invest it in a manner which will keep pace with the inflation by increasing in value or even reliably exceeding the expected rate of inflation. Before you disagree with the inflation rate that we project, there are some things you should know about the way our money is produced. Today it costs the same to print a one-dollar bill as a five-hundred dollar bill. Furthermore, money can be created out of thin air and there are <u>no restrictions</u> any more against such money creation. All backing for the money has been removed.

Another projection is an essential part of our inflation projection. There is a virtual guarantee that, given no restrictions on money creation, <u>money will be created for political objectives</u>. When money is created politically, those who spend it first get all the benefit. It is a hidden tax on money holders or currency hoarders. The <u>first spenders</u> get the <u>benefit</u> because they can buy whatever they wish <u>before</u> prices are <u>bid up</u>. Such <u>spending</u> by those in possession of newly created unbacked money, eventually leads to higher prices after a <u>time lag</u>. If more money is created, money becomes less scarce. As money becomes less scarce, it takes more money to command a fixed amount of goods. Goods become more scarce than money and prices are adjusted upward accordingly. Purchasing power of each individual monetary unit goes down.

What will the coming decade mean to you personally if present policies of money creation are carried to their logical conclusion? It may mean bread selling for a dollar a loaf, an airmail stamp costing a quarter, a $10,000 price on a medium-sized car equipped with the most frequently ordered popular options. It will mean not only obsolescence of the penny (the penny is already obsolete), but also the eventual obsolescence of the nickel and dime.

In making plans for the coming decade, you should have some reasonable estimate of how fast your purchasing power will decline at a given yearly rate of inflation. Here are our computations:

1. At 6% annual inflation your present dollars lose approximately 50% of purchasing power in 12 years.
2. At 7% annual inflation, they lose 50% in 11 years.
3. At 8%, they lose 50% in nine years.
4. At 9%, they lose 50% in eight years.
5. At 10%, they lose 50% in seven and one-third years.

This may shock you. Yet, if the projections of expected rates of inflation over the coming decade are anywhere near accurate, you will lose half of your purchasing power in the time spans detailed above. If the estimates of the inflation rate are accurate, those estimates of loss of half of your purchasing power are strictly mathematical. Hard to believe, isn't it?

ONE WAY TO PROFIT

Folks we know are buying distressed real estate at 10% down and 50¢ to 70¢ on the dollar. Suppose you are presently employed; you shop around on

weekends checking farms, estates, probates, foreclosures, bankruptcies, auctions, and brokers too.

How can you limit risk to tolerable levels?   Let's
take an example. Suppose you find a property appraised
by court at $75,000. Someone has died. The heirs
need and want some money to spend. Assume they are
asking $55,000 cash and that you have $50,000 net
worth. You could get them down to $50,000 for the
property through hard negotiating because they really
want and need to sell. The question is: should you
pay all your $50,000 cash, or should you talk them
into 10% down ($5,000) and the balance over a fifteen
year mortgage?

To limit your risk to tolerable levels, the proper
approach is to push the seller into taking a fifteen year
mortgage, transferable to any new buyer, as 90% of
the purchase price.

Second, the tolerable risk rule says, "Don't enter
any commitment unless you can see at least a potential
100% gain possible over a reasonable period of time."
By using $5,000 down, and remarketing at $65,000 to
$70,000 you should be able to make several hundred
percent profit on your $5,000 down payment.

Let us suppose you can't sell immediately - that
you make tax-deductible interest payments for five
years; you also pay property taxes. (Here is where
it is helpful if the property provides some income to
help carry the payments.) As 1982 rolls around, inflation and the money-supply-expansion have pushed
the appraisal to $135,000. If you sell at the "bargain
price" of $100,000, your original $5,000 down became a capital gain of $50,000 without too much pain
or strain. Furthermore, the sale is easier to make
because more people now recognize inflation taking
place - and you still have ten years to go on a transferable mortgage!

What risk is there on this kind of real estate transaction? If the property has been carefully selected and

negotiated, there isn't very much risk. If the economy goes into a deep depression, you are going to lose your 10% deposit and give up making payments. The heirs will have the property back, plus your deposit and a few payments for their trouble. Remember, however, that you only risked $5,000 out of your starting net worth of $50,000. That means your $45,000 remaining capital has been hiding safely in T-Bills and a few other small ventures. In a depression this $45,000 would provide sharply increased buying power.

On the other hand, if the economy goes into ever steeper inflation, you can pay off that 15-year transferable mortgage in scrip (printing-press money). This kind of transaction might even be suitable on a smaller scale for those young folks who do not have $50,000 liquid net worth to start with, but who do have the twin advantages of Father Time on their side and a regular income from employment. Even if they have only a few thousand in liquid net worth, they can buy a $25,000 property in this manner and start making some real money while charging off the carrying costs of taxes and interest. In this manner they build their net worth very quickly with a definite plan.

The Tolerable Risk rule implies a firm determination on your part not to enter schemes where possible gain or potential profit is less than 100% over a reasonable period of time. In other words, if you can't foresee at least a doubling of your money in three to five years, forget it. Stay out. This rule automatically keeps you out of many risky areas that offer low returns; hence fewer losses.

Limiting risk to Tolerable Levels means you always keep a substantial portion of your capital liquid and ever ready for opportunity. You must not violate this rule! The man who owns a quarter million dollars in real estate, but can't scrape up $1,000 cash, is a violator. Don't follow his example. At times you will have up to 90% of your capital ready for action at certain times in the business cycle.

If you would like to study a little more on the subject, from another point of view, Donald I. Rogers' book, "How To Beat Inflation By Using It," published by Arlington House ($6.95), has a section on real estate as one way of using inflation.

If inflation does not proceed at a 5% to 9% rate over the coming decade, and proceeds at a mere 2% to 4% annual rate, your purchasing power will not decline so fast. Still, your plan will have to include measures to protect yourself against the 2% to 4% rate of inflation yearly. No one can set up a good plan WITHOUT allowing for inflation of significant degree in the coming decade. Whether you are buying insurance, buying real estate, investing in precious stones or rare coins, antiques, or other commitments - it will be necessary to recognize the persistent erosion of your purchasing power that will take place over the next 10 years. Only under the most exceptional circumstances could a situation be envisioned where there was no inflation whatever over the next decade.

How about those folks who have had experience with runaway inflation before, who know how fiat money has a tendency to multiply in a "controlled" economy? These folks think the estimates of inflation over the coming decade are too low. Here, too, any plan that takes into account an inflation rate of 5% to 9% annually presumably will afford a substantial degree of protection against runaway inflation. It is to be hoped that such runaway inflation never does occur for it would mean the total destruction of the existing free world monetary system and present the danger of the establishment of a dictator. After all, it was the trauma of Germany's inflation that set the stage for Hitler.

Chapter 11

WHAT SHOULD YOU BUY?

Good flat buildable land, near utilities, with
water, is always a scarce commodity, especially
when it is on the fringe of a metropolitan area of
500,000 people or more. Good level fringe area
land can yield 25% to 40% capital gains per year on
the payment. Our acreage recommendation is limited to a specific area within 10 miles of metropolitan population concentrations of 500,000 or more.
There may be some good buys near concentrations
of 100,000 or 200,000 people too, but we do not
recommend purchase in those areas. Why? If a
community of 100,000 grows as anticipated and
doubles its population in 10 years, the new population
is only 200,000. That kind of growth does not gobble
up many square miles of land and generate the ter-
rific price pressures you are seeking.

On the other hand, suppose a community of
500,000 grows at the same rate and becomes a community of one million over the same time span? The
price pressures on available land in or near THAT
community are fantastic. The outward move toward
your fringe property is faster, greater, and easier.
It is only in larger metropolitan concentrations that
you will find price competition among the buyers.
What good does it do you to buy land in a small community when there are only two people in the whole
town who MIGHT buy it? In the small-community
situation, you are at the mercy of a limited number
of buyers. But in the big-community situation, you
have the added liquidity generated by many buyers,
rather than just a few. Since land is such an illiquid
investment to begin with (it may take a year or more

78

to sell once you place it on the market), you need all the liquidity help you can get. The only way you can "build in" such liquidity is by planning for it, when you make your original purchase.

There are a lot of areas around the country that are prime purchase speculations right now. A few examples are: east of Houston, between Dallas and Ft. Worth, northeast of El Paso, between El Paso and Las Cruces, in the Chicago-Aurora-Joliet triangle, west of Milwaukee, along the Washington-Baltimore Parkway, south of Arlington, between Phoenix and Tucson, south of Minneapolis, west of Detroit, or in California, south of Newport Beach, north of Ventura, north of San Francisco. There are a dozen more areas and if you study for a while, you could name many more near you.

It is always best to try to get future commercial frontage, if possible, by paying a little more. It does not matter that the business district may now be five to 10 miles away.

Don't buy from large land companies or high-pressure salesmen! Many are unabashed promotions selling land out in the boondocks, away from the shops, the jobs and the people. There are more "sharks" on the California mainland than there are cruising off the coast - and many brokers will verify that some are working in land. Your best buy will probably be from a private party who may have listed his parcel with a country broker. Don't be afraid to contact at least a dozen brokers before you buy. Their offices are relatively empty now and they are quite willing to work to earn their commissions.

Pay a little more, if necessary, to get blacktop frontage. The parcels you want are already served by good roads - not out in the middle of some barren area. Those parcels on the roads increase in value the soonest. As emphasized before, buy a big enough piece. A half acre or less is much too small.

CORE-CITY PROPERTY

When clients approach real estate brokers for the first time and request properties that can be purchased 20% to 50% below market, most brokers immediately offer them core-city properties in declining neighborhoods. These are the properties that can often be purchased well below last year's appraisal. One question remains: should you buy them?

Let us define terms first, so that everyone has a clear idea and sound basis for decision making. By CORE-CITY properties we mean: properties in older parts of the city or metropolitan area that were built 20 to 100 years ago, usually within one to 20 miles of the city center. By FRINGE-AREA properties we mean: properties located within 30 minutes driving distance of the nearest city job concentration perimeter. Remember that we are speaking of major metropolitan areas now with population concentrations of a half million or more.

To choose the best possible area, you need a map of the metropolitan area and a dark pencil. With the pencil, circle the core area, the center of the city, the older area, the older neighborhoods. Within that circle are properties in which you WILL NOT be interested. Take the pencil again and circle the perimeter of the metropolitan concentration. You now have a second wider circle showing where your search should begin. Taking your pencil again, draw a third circle at the limit of 30-minutes driving time from job areas. That is where your search ends. Your largest circle is now your outer boundary (30-minute driving time area). Your middle circle is your inner search boundary and your inside and smallest circle, the core-city circle, represents the area in which you will not be interested under any circumstances. Note what you have done. You have isolated for yourself, and any brokers you talk to,

potential geographical listing areas. Take the map
with you when you contact brokers and you will save
both parties a great deal of time and words, and you
will make your bargain searching three times as
efficient.   This little technique normally silences
brokers who would push you into declining neighborhoods, deteriorating urban areas, etc.

The safest areas then, from both an investment
and personal standpoint, are the areas between the
two outer circles on your map.

Since the housing shortage is greatest among the
welfare groups, the initial thrust of public housing
will probably take place in the cities.   Low-income
groups won't have the income necessary to generate
housing profits, so public inner-city housing probably
won't be the profit-maker.   Medium and higher income groups (especially wage earners, families with
children) will most likely center their demands for
housing in the suburbs and beyond the city.   That is
where your profit-making attention should focus.
Who can possibly make a profit out of inner-city
property except some contractor?   Even the best
of public housing projects usually turn into slums in
a few years.   Low-income housing almost automatically seems to attract irresponsible tenants who
quickly or gradually often turn excellent properties
into residential horrors.   Even in those rare instances where it might be possible to make money in
inner-city residential housing, municipal tax struc-
tures are becoming distinctly oppressive.

For your own profit and benefit you must distinguish (1) between so-called bargains based on last
year's appraisals where the market price has DE-
CLINED, and (2) true bargains based on last year's
appraisal where the market price has INCREASED.
You must identify the neighborhood trend on any
listing and avoid the losers if you wish to make good
profits.   It is far, far better to buy in a poor

suburban neighborhood, where the buildings will soon be torn down for commercial development, than it is to buy in a core-city area which may be the beneficiary of a new federal housing development.

There are many good buys in the fringe areas; forget about tract houses. Many developers have the gall to put a $40,000 or $45,000 house on a postage-stamp size lot far out amidst farmers' fields! If your PERSONAL real estate commitment is going to take shape as a house purchase, insist on at least 15,000 square feet in the lot (100' x 150' minimum). That is your minimum target. You will never regret having the additional land and the bigger the better. If you are going to "hock it" anyway, you might as well have the land added to the mortgage. Having land means you can resell pieces later as the land rises in value. The developers are apparently cutting corners on land, just as auto manufacturers seem to be cutting corners on warranties and guarantees.

Stay out of fashionable areas or already developed areas. You must ANTICIPATE the crowd, not join the crowd that has already arrived. It is most important that you consider properties beyond the edge of presently developed metropolitan areas. You want the property where the town will extend five years from now. There are too many bidders for property that is already fully developed and in fashionable areas. These additional bidders will compete against you, pay more money, and prevent you from buying property below market.

In residential or commercial properties that are vacant, the opportunities for making money are great. Instead of looking for rentable properties to purchase that are fully occupied, it is suggested that you start looking at good vacant properties that have some sort of problem. The world pays very high for the services of problem-solvers. People who can consistently solve difficult complex problems, problems that are not run-of-the-mill, can present big demands to the world and have them met.

Amazingly enough, a property that is vacant, that has some kind of problem, usually scares off most real estate speculators and investors. While the problems are often not run-of-the-mill, they can be solved by almost any individual with a little capital, a little elbow grease, and a willingness to attack the problem. Don't buy unsound construction. Today, however, in most metropolitan areas one can hire skilled workers - tree surgeons, experienced landscape gardeners, inside and outside painters, plasterers, carpenters, for $100 to $1,000 per job who are experienced in solving most any problem one can encounter. Much of this work can be contracted for as little as $4 to $5 an hour and sometimes much less. Many sound vacant rentable properties have a problem of this nature, a readily solvable one. Usually it turns out that the original owner didn't have sufficient CONFIDENCE in the property to invest the limited amount of money necessary to solve the problem, or else he tried it himself and botched the job. Such a situation is a SET-UP for the smart speculator. The owner is probably discouraged, disillusioned, confused, somewhat broke, or perhaps lacks confidence in his own property.

You can solve all these problems for him and take him out of this turmoil by purchasing the property at a very favorable price and often on very favorable financial terms where the owner takes back a second mortgage. Surprisingly enough, many real estate brokers will only show you readily occupiable or fully occupied properties. If you want to try your hand at solving some of the simpler problems with vacant properties, chances are you will have to insist on seeing such properties, or the broker will not

show them to you. He probably passed them by <u>too</u>
when he was looking over the listings.

One point that should be emphasized is: when
you go to solve <u>whatever</u> problem exists, that you
know <u>precisely</u> what you are doing and have the complete array of equipment necessary to solve the
problem if you are going to attempt it yourself.
<u>Don't</u> try to remove giant trees, for instance, unless
you have all the equipment and skill necessary for a
quick job. We discovered, for example, reliable
firms willing to contract a truck plus two experienced
men, plus all the necessary equipment for a paltry
$9 an hour. One or two days work of an experienced
crew may turn a vacant seedy property into a desirable rentable building worth several thousand dollars
more.

Here are some tips to save you money and make
you money in fixing up property:

1. Always get competitive bids on any job over
   $100. There are <u>no exceptions</u> - no matter
   how well you know your first contact.
2. Have people bid by the job, not by the hour.
   A plumber who gives you a $4.50 an hour bid
   and takes 20 hours to do a $50 job, is no bar-
   gain. Contract professional work by the
   job, not by the hour.
3. Use moonlighting labor where you can. A
   plumber who works full time during the day
   for a large plumbing firm may well be willing to do a job for you on a weekend for half
   price. Use him. Often he will have moonlighting friends in other building trades and
   similar professions. If he proves satisfactory, ask him to make recommendations of
   his friends. It won't matter that he does the
   job on a weekend if you are a regularly employed entrepreneur anyway. If you are
   speculating in real estate as a profitable

experience in addition to your regular job,
you will want to inspect the work while you
are home on weekends.

4. <u>Always</u> <u>inspect</u> <u>work</u> <u>in</u> <u>progress.</u> No exceptions.

5. Never pay for a job in advance or without inspection. No exceptions. If you must make
   a deposit, make it a small one.

6. Use high school or summer student labor for
   unskilled work. This can be cutting lawns,
   washing windows, simple landscaping and
   other "muscle" jobs. Never use unskilled
   labor without being there to supervise. No
   exceptions. They may "goof off", wasting
   your time slurping cokes, etc. There is a
   vast pool of unskilled labor available around
   the minimum wage-rate levels, but you will
   have to <u>be</u> <u>there</u> and <u>keep</u> the <u>jobs</u> <u>moving</u> to
   use it profitably.

One college professor says, "People in my area
seem to have a great deal of success in this type of
venture. According to the scheme, the house is
bought and immediately rented out. The rent payments pay off the mortgage payments and also the
initial down payment. As inflation continues the
rent payments keep increasing while mortgage payments stay the same. In a college town, it is not
difficult to get a conscientious professor-type as a
renter who would take excellent care of the house."

Not only will inflation's progress enable you to
raise rents every year or second year, but it will
insure that the value of your property rises constantly. The professor has the right idea and right now
is an excellent time to obtain mortgage financing.
It is necessary to "shop" your mortgage - don't accept the first interest rate figure thrown at you.
One-half percent difference in interest rate on any

new mortgage can mean many thousands of dollars over the life of the mortgage.

There is a way to make the professor's idea work overtime to multiply your profits and capital gains. That way is to buy residential houses where the neighborhood is turning commercial on a busy street. Business streets are often quite noisy and you will discover many of the houses along such streets are for sale, perhaps already vacant, or the owner is "itching" to move out if he could just find a buyer. Solve his problem and put some money in your pocket. Best searching areas are within a block or two of current new suburban shopping centers on busy streets. While people looking for a house to buy see a busy noisy street as a disadvantage, those looking for a house to rent are not so fussy, particularly if they have kids. Noise is of no consequence whatever to them.

This is not a recommendation to buy core city property. Only fringe area property or suburban residential housing, where the neighborhood will be going commercial within a sixty month period. Corner properties are best but they may be too high-priced already. Check the property right next door to the corner lot. If an oil company wants to put up a gas station it will need two or three lots at a noisy, high-traffic intersection, not just the corner lot.

Always buy where the trend is up - not down.

Chapter 12

SELECTING A BROKER

Should you really SELECT a broker that you will work with for a long time? Most folks just grab at listings rather than trying to make an exact procedure out of selecting a broker. Does it cost you extra money when you buy through a broker? A very important question.

Brokers are all over the place. For example, one out of every 131 California residents is a licensed Realtor. This does not include many thousands of people working on commission in the field under the umbrella of someone else's license. Brokers are just as plentiful in other states as they are in California (Florida, for example).

Successful real estate property speculation consists not only of properly evaluating properties, but also of properly evaluating the people who are handling the deal for you. The broker you want to select is one who will work for you as a buyer. By all the legal rules, etc., the broker is supposed to represent the seller all of the time, but that just isn't the way it works out. Many brokers actually LET the seller take a lower price (when he had an awareness of the fact that the buyer was willing to pay a higher price), on the same exact terms. One man, very active in the real estate field for many years, has estimated that at least 50% of a broker's effort on the average listing consists of hammering the seller down to a marketable level.

With so many licensed people active in the field, competitions to obtain listings - particularly in good areas - often become very, very fierce. There are brokers who seek to accumulate the biggest pile of listings without a great deal of concern for the quality or saleability of the listings. There are other brokers who are less enthusiastic in accepting listings and who try to obtain only saleable listings, properties that are listed at market levels or less, not ahead of the market. Work with the second type of individual who handles a smaller number of listings where most of the fat has already been squeezed out of the price. This is in direct contrast to brokers who take listings on "dreams."

Who pays the broker's commission? The seller. When you are a buyer, you don't have to pay the broker's commission, so why not use his valuable services? They cost you nothing and give you a valuable intermediary, one you could not hire or motivate quickly on any other basis on such short notice. He wants to help you, the buyer, to get the property you want at the price you want to pay and under the terms you want. If he cannot satisfy your needs his pockets remain empty. He MUST satisfy the needs of the buyer or he will never have a regular income.

Smart brokers recognize the value of potential speculator-investor clients. When you are searching out a broker who will work with you, you must be alert to his recognition of the value of your continuing relationship. If he seems to be a "one-shot Charlie," forget him. Build a substantial relationship that you expect to last for many years with someone who will appreciate your continuing good will.

It is not enough to "view and appraise" property alone. The broker you are working with is your representative, even though the seller is paying the commission. The better you learn how to use his skills, work with him, and take advantage of his value as an intermediary, his experience, his negotiating ability (this is a must), the more profit you will make. A broker who satisfies your needs and has these abilities will bring you deal after deal, time after time. The "one-shot Charlie," on the other hand, may help you through one profitable deal but forget you next year when some lucrative deal comes his way.

NEED TO SELL

There is one more qualification a broker MUST have for you to work with him well and make consistent profits, and this one qualification is more important than all the rest for a speculator. The broker must IDENTIFY the NEED TO SELL.

The buyer and the broker who identify the need to sell and help get the property sold do the seller a favor. They fill the identified need quickly in a market that is usually slow and sluggish, particularly where problem properties are concerned. For helping the seller in this manner they often get a better price and/or better terms than Mr. Average Buyer.

If the broker doesn't have any idea of how badly the seller wants to move the property, this is not the man for you. The kind of broker you are searching out instinctively identifies the need for a quick sale, or a certain kind of sale, or a high-cash-down sale, or an estate sale that can be consummated well below conservative appraisal. Piling up a wide selection of listings is only a small part of the job. The important thing is that he have listings that can make you money! These brokers are rare. Perhaps only one in 20, or one in 50, consistently and regularly tries to identify the need to sell on every listing he handles. This is probably the most important information on a property that a buyer could have - next to careful inspection of the property itself. Listed prices mean little in such cases where the broker has identified the need to sell.

In your property hunting you should not only isolate a broker who identifies the need to sell all listings, but also check out carefully properties where the need to sell is imperative. Do not be scared away by a listing price that seems remote from the price you wish to pay. If the broker does not have this information there is no way you can have this information and deal through the broker. Since it is one of the major keys to success in property speculation, only by your broker having and providing you with this information will it be in your possession. While you get the advantage or reward of a better price, better terms, or better profit by providing liquidity and identifying the need to sell, the broker is also rewarded. He gets quicker and more frequent commissions.

When you become a speculator and join the ranks of other speculators, you widen the bidding for properties that have a need to be sold. More bidders for various properties mean better prices for the sellers. The more speculators there are, the better price the sellers, in any given area, will realize. In fact, those who have the need to sell may themselves be recent speculators, who have had their wings clipped by speculating unwisely.

The need to sell can originate from many sources. It might be an heir who needs money from an inheritance which contains a hard-to-sell property. It could arise from an imminent foreclosure by a lender who is going to take over a property. (When you deal with foreclosures you often help the seller get out a substantial portion of his equity, money he might not realize for himself if the lender forecloses.) The need to sell could arise from a state sale, or an estate sale; it could arise because someone is moving or is transferred, from a divorce, a marriage, from capital needs generated by another business, or because the seller merely wants money to play the market. It may be that the seller doesn't like a neighbor, he is too far from a school, too near a school, that he prefers to move immediately into an apartment, and so on.

The broker who doesn't find out <u>why</u> the <u>seller</u> <u>wants</u> to <u>sell</u> may not be able to negotiate the price you want to pay. Remember those three little letters - WHY. Remember to ask <u>how</u> <u>soon</u> the sale must be consummated. Your inspection time, as a busy person, is limited. You cannot waste your time inspecting EVERY listing a broker has. This will pinpoint properties for your inspection in a much quicker and more efficient manner.

A WORD OF CAUTION

The last few paragraphs should help you pinpoint from one to six brokers with whom you can work well. At the same time you are evaluating properties your mental computer should also be studying the broker carefully. You will be successful in isolating good brokers to work with if you follow the instructions.

When you do find a good broker, however, you must beware of the tendency to become over-confident in his ability. Suppose you have two transactions with him and they both turn into nice chunks of profits. He may call you on a third property, tell you the deal must be accomplished in 48 hours and you may be too busy to inspect and evaluate it personally. Do NOT, under any circumstances, buy property you have not personally inspected. Don't fail to tread upon every inch of any property which you buy. There are NO EXCEPTIONS to this rule - no matter how good your broker and no matter how many profits he has turned for you in the past. Motto: If you can't afford the time to inspect it carefully, you can't afford the money to buy it.

Once you have selected one or more fine brokers you must try to cooperate with them when they bring you a hot deal. Inspect it promptly. Make an offer promptly if it appeals to you. Don't dilly-dally for

eight weeks making up your mind. That will not enhance your ability with them. It is a team relationship. You are the one who makes the big chunk of
money and benefits most from top-notch buys.

Do you have certain types of property that you
wish to consider, such as houses with potential commercial frontage? Do you have a minimum land area
in mind? Is there only one kind of construction you
prefer (such as stone or brick), and are there other
types you will not buy, such as frame? Is there a
minimum potential profit, a cut-off point, where you
would not be interested in properties that promise
to return you less (say $10,000)? Is there a certain
kind of neighborhood in which you will not buy (a
deteriorating neighborhood, as opposed to neighborhoods with a rising trend)? Are there certain
clauses you want in any loan or mortgage contract
you sign (such as the transferability clause)?

You will help your selected brokers immensely
if you <u>write</u> all these things <u>out</u> on a piece of paper
ahead of time and give it to him. In fact, for a few
dollars you can have a hundred copies of your special
requirements printed up. This is to your advantage
as well as the broker's. A broker will find it very
difficult to waste your time inspecting unqualified
listings or properties if he has your list of requirements <u>staring</u> him in the face.

Chapter 13

HOW TO NEGOTIATE

Knowing how to negotiate a successful real estate deal is as important as knowing what property to buy. This short course in negotiating should save you thousands upon thousands of dollars if you carefully study and follow these rules. Your first attempts to follow them may be a bit clumsy because you aren't used to them, but don't become discouraged. By the time you follow these rules in your third negotiation, you will already be a more highly skilled negotiator than 90% of the population. Use them well.

1. At first, don't drive too hard of a bargain. Get the other party involved before you get tough. Get him to start thinking in terms of what you can do for him. Approach him as though you are a problem solver. Remember, in a negotiation, the other party is technically your opponent, but you won't get very far if you treat him as an opponent. First, you must get him to realize what problems you can solve for him, how you can solve them, and get him to make some kind of psychological or monetary commitment. For example, if you are trying to rent a house to someone, get him to talk to his present landlord about canceling his present lease. The other party's action in approaching his present landlord to cancel a lease, is the beginning of a successful negotiation for the rental of your place.

2. Find out what the other party wants, for successful negotiation. If you do not know what he wants, both monetarily and psychologically, you do not know what to offer him. In wheeling and dealing in foreclosures in real estate, for example,

93

sometimes the other party merely wants out of an intolerable situation. In this case, the psychological consideration is more important than the monetary consideration. If you can't solve the other party's psychological needs, merely offering him more money won't get the job done.

3. Put it in writing - while the other party is enthused. That great deal that the other party likes so well can cool quickly if a relative gets to him, or if the banker throws cold water on the deal. No negotiating meeting should close without both parties writing down and making notes on what they have, at least tentatively, agreed upon so far. Emphasize the positive points of agreement. A firm and factual agreement, legal and binding, is better than a tentative agreement, especially if you can get it in the first part of the negotiation. Put it in writing. Don't depend on faith. Don't expect the other party to be as enthusiastic a month from now, or even a day from now, as he is right at this moment. Other people may be quick to discourage him. They will dash cold water on the deal (sometimes out of pure jealousy, envy, or greed), and you will not be present to uphold your case.

4. Once an agreement has been reached, go home! Hang up! Get out! Don't rehash! Don't take unnecessary chances when you have your deal. Salesmen will verify that many good orders have been blown sky high by a salesman hanging around and talking too much after an agreement has been reached.

5. If you have something in your hand - take it! Don't procrastinate. If the other party wants to give you a check today, take it today and cash it today. Don't wait. Don't expect it to be good tomorrow after his friends, relatives, and others get at him. Businessmen know that one way to cut down the number of hot checks and "stop payment" checks

is to deposit them within hours after they receive them.

In every negotiation, if it is to be legal, at least one dollar should change hands. Get to that stage early in the game, even if it is only a token amount (for example, a $5 deposit for the present owner of a property being foreclosed, which you give him in return for a signed option to buy his equity in the property for a specified amount). On the following page is a typical deposit receipt which may be used for this purpose.

6. Don't loan money to friends. This is an inviolable rule and the quickest way possible to lose both friends and money. If you must loan money to a friend, get a signed note from him for the loan. At least this will give you a tax deduction for a bad debt if the guy never pays you back. All loans to anyone should always be supported by a written note, be they friend, relative, or business acquaintance. That's the only way the IRS will allow a tax deduction on a bad debt.

If a friend is in need and you want to help him, go ahead and help him, or make him an outright gift. As a potentially successful negotiator, you lose your negotiating ability in a deal where you loan money to a friend. You retain your negotiating ability when you give something to a friend.

7. Negotiate only on your home ground. When serious negotiations are in order, make the other party come to you, to your own home or your own office. Naturally, when you are dealing in real estate, you may often conduct initial interviews at the site. When it gets down to the actual negotiating session, however, after the initial interviews, get them on your ground, not theirs. This gives you a psychological advantage. If you are in a strange city, all hotels can rent you a sitting room or a suite, by the hour or by the day, for a very nominal

DEPOSIT RECEIPT

_____19 . . .

        CITY   STATE

RECEIVED FROM _____

the sum of _____ Dollars

as a deposit on account of the purchase price of the following de-

scribed property, situated in the _____

County of _____,

State of _____to-wit:

subject to conditions, restrictions, reservations, easements, and
rights-of-way now of record,

for the purchase price of _____ Dollars

The balance of the purchase price to be paid as follows:

AND IT IS HEREBY AGREED:

SELLER SO DESIGNATES BY   BUYER SO DESIGNATES BY
AUTHORIZED SIGNATURES   AUTHORIZED SIGNATURES

_____   _____

_____   _____

_____   _____

charge. Get the other party to a neutral place. If you can't get him to your own home ground, get him out of his area.

8. Don't be penny-wise when it comes to an attorney. The attorney need not be brought into preliminary negotiations, but when you have a tough deal worth many thousands of dollars, all ready to go, pay the attorney his pound of flesh and have him draw it up. Have your attorney send the deal to the other party's attorney, or to the other party. Remember, your attorney sends it to his attorney. Your attorney draws up the documents. Don't permit his attorney to draw up the documents and send to your attorney. This gives you added psychological leverage.

9. Don't enter into any agreement unless there is a "trap door" clause. If something goes wrong, you want to be able to walk away. In dealing in property under threat of foreclosure, for example, you lay out a small amount of money, say $5 or $20, for the option to purchase owner's equity. If the deal sours later on, your loss is a few dollars - you haven't laid out a big amount of cash. When you borrow money on a property, for instance, you don't get co-signers for the loan, or pledge other personal assets and personal holdings you may have, as collateral. You do not endanger your other holdings for the sake of one deal you are negotiating. The only thing you endanger is your deposit or down payment.

10. Negotiate only when you are emotionally calm and in good physical health. Don't negotiate when you are distraught, disgusted, or disturbed. Avoid the three "d's." If you must negotiate under those emotional conditions, get someone to do it for you.

11. The value of anything depends on whether you are buying or selling. It quickly becomes apparent in successful negotiations who has the most to

gain and who has to make a move. You retain the advantage if you emphasize the importance of the other fellow's objective. He may not (and often should not) realize or concentrate upon your particular objectives. You are solving his problem; don't let him get the idea that you need him more than he needs you (for successful negotiations).

Evaluate your opponent carefully and take stock of his customary regional, racial, or geographical differences. Don't try to rush the patient Oriental or the St. Louis Dutchman. On the other hand, move along rapidly with the enthusiastic, fast-talking Italian - don't lag behind or you will discourage him. You are complimenting the other fellow's racial origin or geographical customs when you recognize them, acknowledge them, and make allowances in your own approach for them. It is one of the highest forms of compliment one can pay.

12. Don't try to second guess your opponent. Power doesn't mean anything if the other person doesn't know he has the power. Don't bring the fact of his power out into the open, particularly when you are dealing with giant-sized lenders, bankers, corporations, or individuals. Get that negotiation on a person-to-person, individual-to-individual track. Otherwise you will find yourself negotiating against the "system" - an unequal opponent.

13. People who go into a negotiation with higher goals always come out ahead. Don't start with what you feel are reasonable goals. You can always lower them to "reasonable" levels later. Shoot for the big one. When pricing property, price it attractively but not ridiculously below market. While everyone likes to save a dollar, people get suspicious if something is too cheap or too easy to accomplish.

14. Let the opponent make the first concession to set the tone for the negotiation. It can be a meaningless concession but get him to make it anyway.

(Example: get him to throw in the present torn draperies if you buy his house). Get that first concession and get it early; it gets the other party used to the idea of making concessions and gets him in the proper habit pattern.

15. Sometimes it pays to be unreasonable, and irrational. Stop conceding occasionally. Never begin a negotiation on what you consider fair grounds. Ask for more when you are selling. Begin by offering less when you are buying. You can always move in the other party's direction, but it is often impossible to retreat.

16. Make certain your negotiating plan has some "give-ups." The other party won't feel satisfied that he has made a good negotiation unless he has won some points from you. Unless you stick in a contract a few things you expect to lose, you will have to concede important points. Therefore, stick in a few unimportant "give-ups" intentionally, at the beginning of the negotiation. For example, if the seller of a property is willing to carry a second mortgage at 9% interest, and you would be willing to have him carry a 7% interest second mortgage, begin by offering him 5% interest (not 7%)! Let him "win" those two percentage points of interest from you at a crucial point in the negotiation. Everyone likes to feel they are a winner. Make sure your negotiation plan has at least three to six "give-up" items. Dole them out as you feel the need so that you don't have to give away more crucial items.

17. Use "trade-offs." If your opponent mentions he wants something, always ask something else from him in return. Don't just say, "sure," and then hit him with a bomb you expect an hour later. Make it a trading process, not one of unparalleled generosity one minute, and demanding unreasonableness the next.

18. Work toward the best time to deal, the time when the burden will be on the other party to get the deal through. Timing is important. In a foreclosure, for example, the best time to negotiate is within 72 hours before the lender sends the sheriff. You set up your deal well in advance, of course, but you don't really worry about hard-rock negotiations until the other party has already committed himself and is working on a definite time schedule. The most important time of negotiating is the last 15 minutes. That's where the concessions are made! Don't be an "easy touch" during those last few minutes. Give up only what you absolutely must to clinch the deal. Be super alert those last 15 minutes. Put the timing in your favor!

Chapter 14

BUYING FORECLOSURES

<u>THE MORAL ISSUE: SHOULD YOU BUY FORECLOS-</u>
<u>URES AT ALL?</u>

Some feel that they are better off to pay retail
for a <u>new</u> house for, say $40,000, than trying to buy
a similar house several years old, say for $25,000,
at foreclosure auction. What if some <u>poor soul</u> is
being thrown out of his home?! Isn't this "mean"?!

First, at a foreclosure auction, the LENDER IS
already the OWNER. He has complied with the law
and when <u>lender forecloses</u> (not you), the previous
owner loses any equity completely. The lender usually
bids the price of the trust deed (example $25,000 trust
deed on $40,000 house). If you bid above lender's bid
(including foreclosure cost), any EXCESS funds, in
most states, are to be RETURNED TO the PREVIOUS
OWNER. In other words, if you bid $30,000 and lender
only bids $25,000, $5,000 would have to be returned
to previous owner as excess equity. Even if you bid
only $1,000 or a few hundred dollars over lender's
bid, the previous owner is better off. With you as
bidder, previous owner gets SOMETHING! With the
LENDER as BIDDER, previous owner gets NOTHING!
At that point in time he has already relinquished ownership of the property. Therefore, previous owner is
better off if you bid than if you do NOT bid. <u>Your</u>
<u>refusal to participate</u> will actually <u>cost previous owner</u>
<u>money</u> and leave a black mark for bad loan on his
credit record. Your bid can wipe out that black mark
against his credit and sometimes return equity to
previous owner. Remember that bank or lender is
quite likely to make money if they are permitted to
own the property, by bidding the amount of the loan

plus costs. Example: Two years ago a broker
showed us a $52,000 house that the lender had just
foreclosed on a $39,000 mortgage. We went to
lender with an offer of $45,000! We felt certain
that $6,000 over the $39,000 foreclosure cost would
be fat profit for lender-owned home, plus several
thousands for broker's commission. LENDER
REFUSED OUR OFFER of $45,000! Said he preferred
to hold property and try to get over $50,000, well
above the foreclosed price lender paid! If lender got
$50,000 after foreclosure auction, previous owner
who had been foreclosed would get nothing, not even
one dollar! Therefore, it is better that you bid on a
property at the time of the foreclosure, in excess of
lender's bid, than not bid at all. One way or another,
that property will be remarketed sooner or later, at
higher prices. YOU might as well do the remarketing
and make the PROFIT INSTEAD of the LENDER who
foreclosed. After all, he is not supposed to be in the
real estate business!

The biggest secret of making money in real
estate is to buy cheaply. Foreclosures can be bought
cheaper than almost any other kind of property.

ADD LIQUIDITY - BUY NEED-TO-SELL DEALS

If you are going into real estate, which is illiquid
anyway, you want to buy it cheap so you can sell it at
a competitive price when the time comes to sell, and
still make a sizeable profit. Property you have for
sale, at prices below market, is more liquid, in
general, than the same property priced at full ticket.
Therefore, you buy cheap to sell below market, but
still make a substantial profit, if the need-to-sell on
your part should arise. On the other hand, if the
need-to-sell does not arise, and you acquire the property cheaply, hopefully way below market, you can
remarket it leisurely at full ticket, or even offer it
above market, in the hopes that a buyer will pay your

price! That is the purpose for being interested in
foreclosures -- added liquidity -- lower prices --
lowered risks -- increased chances of substantial
capital gains on turnover -- higher income.

Foreclosure properties can take many forms.
They can be 2-bedroom houses, 7-bedroom houses
with swimming pools and tennis courts, farms,
ranches, acreage, commercial buildings -- you name
it -- someone is not paying the loan on it today and
is close to imminent foreclosure! Where property
must be sold -- that's where you have the opportunity
to get the greatest bargains.

Properties that need not be sold or are under no
time pressure to sell are usually unlikely to be priced
far below market. In fact, if you talk to brokers a
lot, you discover that most properties are priced
either above market, or at least at full market. Very
seldom is a steady stream of properties priced below
market. In the Los Angeles area, for example, when
a property is priced below market through a broker,
frequently it sells within one day to one week! Then
the brokers are stuck with their over-priced load of
listings until another candidate comes along.

RECORD-BUSTERS! OBSTACLES CAN BE   AN ADVANTAGE

Foreclosures are increasing in all categories, in
all states. Never have there been such record-
breaking numbers of unpaid loans, loans in default,
and properties foreclosed in the last two decades!
Rest assured, it is happening in YOUR area -- some
loans are not being paid, and the properties are going
to be repossessed by the lender and resold. It is
happening -- so the foreclosures are there for those
of you who PERSEVERE in spite of obstacles. When
you go after foreclosures, remember that obstacles
are an advantage, not a disadvantage! Think positive.
The harder it is to get the legal information, to check

out the taxes, to negotiate with owner or forecloser,
the less competition there will be for that property!
The more obstacles, the less competition on bidding,
the better for you! So don't be deterred by OBSTA-
CLES. The more, the better! Once you learn how to
overcome the obstacles in searching out and finding
foreclosures, you'll have significant advantage over
the people who don't know these details. Therefore,
don't be stopped, don't regret the time you spend
learning how foreclosures are handled in your state
and in your county. Don't be put off by the terms.
(Consult the chapter at the end of this book which
carries a glossary of real estate terminology that
will be helpful to you, terms in usage in the industry.)

THREE CHANCES FOR YOU ON MOST DEALS!
        What are your 3 basic ways to buy foreclosed
property below market? They are, in chronological
order: (1) dealing with the owner who is being foreclosed, (2) buying at the foreclosure auction (sometimes called a trustee auction or lender's auction),
and (3) dealing direct with the lender after the lender
forecloses on a property, and lender is the new owner.
Note that if you fail to acquire a property through the
owner's being foreclosed, you have two MORE
CHANCES at that same property: at the foreclosure
auction itself, or dealing with the lender if lender is
high bidder at the foreclosure auction! What are
some of the advantages and disadvantages to each
method of acquiring property in foreclosure?
        Method (1) - DEALING DIRECT WITH THE
PARTY BEING FORECLOSED. You can frequently
roll over the financing. That is, it might take only
$1500 to $5000 cash for you to begin to acquire your
first house or other property this way. Why should
an owner deal with you, rather than with a broker?
Why should an owner be motivated to deal with you,
rather than let the property go back to the lender

(usually a bank or savings and loan)? The answer is you get money to this party -- money he would not get otherwise. Briefly summarized, you are going to put some cash in the owner's pocket, money he can use to relocate and also to save his credit. Credit is very important to any party in financial trouble, and saving someone's credit rating is a wonderfully useful social service, in case the owner wants to buy a house, or business or something else on credit later on. Those are the two things you can do for an owner being forclosed -- put cash in his pocket to relocate, and help save his credit. A third thing you can do for him is help him out of a difficult and often intolerable situation; relieve him of pressing responsibilities, give him a chance to get on his feet again. You have these things going in your favor once the property is in default.

In every state there are properties going into default, where loans are not being paid. Yes, the legal terminology might be slightly different, but where you are talking about potential 4-figure, 5-figure and even 6-figure profits, it is worth your while to spend a little time learning the legal terms used in your state. It is also worthwhile for you to chase down those properties, however they are described, published, auctioned, and re-acquired by others. Do not be DETERRED by seemingly difficult-sounding unfamiliar obstacles. Sometimes, in dealing with clerks at a county recorder's office, you may find that you have to ask PRECISELY the right question in order to get the right answer. Therefore, go down, learn the terms, find out where the notices are published or posted, and get ready to deal with owners, trustees, or even new owners after foreclosure.

There are four major sources of foreclosure properties. The first is the real estate broker. If a broker is a specialist in foreclosures, chances are he can put you on to some good deals. If he is not,

you are likely to be wasting your time with him. He
will be trying to sell those properties at full ticket,
as much as he can get, a figure that includes his 6%
commission. If you can find a broker you can work
with on foreclosures, fine. It will require some
prospecting on your part. Maybe one in 50 brokers
will qualify. If you do not find such a broker, read on.

A second source of foreclosures is your banker.
Banks have a certain number of their mortgage loans
turn bad. They foreclose. They call these properties
"REO's" (real estate owned). They don't like to talk
about these because REO's are mistakes they have
made. If your banker is friendly, this is a good
source. We have found wide variance in bankers
willing to tell you about REO's. It is important to
build good bank relationships. Over a period of years,
REO's become a fringe benefit of such a relationship.
No relationship, no REO's.

Savings and loans are also a good source of foreclosed properties. They have more REO's than banks.
Sometimes they are a little more willing to tell you
about them than the banker, but not much. If you work
with savings and loans, pump them for REO's. If not,
forget the savings and loans.

The very best source for properties in the process of foreclosure, or to be sold at foreclosure sales,
is your county court house. Those records have to be
filed by the county clerk -- and that is where your
broker gets his information. In most major metropolitan areas, all the legal work is done for you by a
publication. Almost every major metropolitan area
has a legal newspaper, a newspaper publishing foreclosure notices, sale notices, credit, court suits,
tax liens, judgments, new incorporations, and all
similar data taken from legal records. The content
of such a newspaper will be very limited. Las Vegas
has such a paper. Los Angeles has such a paper,
San Diego has such a paper, and so do most other

cities. Ask your attorney or look in the Yellow Pages.

Subscription to these papers is usually quite high - around $5 a month. Subscribe for one month rather than taking a year's subscription. (What are you going to do with 5,000 notices of foreclosure?) Test it for a month and chances are you will have more properties than you can inspect and evaluate. That is where your broker gets his information.

To summarize briefly: Best source of foreclosures is your LEGAL newspaper; in the unusual event your area doesn't have a legal newspaper, just march down to the court house yourself. It will take you 20 minutes of fumbling around but you will find out who to go to and how to get the information quickly and efficiently.

In the past, lenders used to let payments run six to eight months late before filing notice of foreclosure. That's all changed since 1966. Now, if payments run two to three months late, bang! "The Notice of Default" is filed.

LENDERS ACQUIRE PROPERTY TWO WAYS

There are two main routes to foreclosure proceedings. The first is the ordinary formal foreclosure route taken through the courts. This is a lengthy, involved process and may take a couple of years. Without getting into a lot of legal gibberish, let it suffice to say that most lenders do not utilize this first method. It is clumsy, lengthy and expensive to foreclose on properties in this manner. Very seldom will you be dealing with lenders' foreclosures that have proceeded through the courts, as lenders do not like to go that route. They have a short cut.

The second route to a lender's foreclosing on a property is called the "TRUSTEE SALE" method. This method is relatively simple and inexpensive compared with the first. A "Notice of Default" is filed after several mortgage payments are missed!

Ninety days after the notice of default is filed, a "Notice of Trustee Sale" is filed. Approximately 30 to 60 days after notice is filed, the property will be sold for whatever it will bring at a "Trustee Sale" auction. The <u>lender</u> (who holds the defaulted mortgage) actually conducts the trustee auction to sell the property to high bidder after original owner fails to come up with the money. If the lender holds a $17,000 mortgage on a $30,000 property, he will normally bid the full amount of the mortgage. Anyone who bids over the amount of the mortgage will get it -- providing he is high bidder and the court approves. Short, simple, easy! By the time the property reaches this stage, the seller has lost all his equity completely. He is going to lose it with or without you, so you are not "taking advantage" of him. On the contrary, by widening the bidding you may help him to regain some equity and get money he would not otherwise realize.

CERTAIN STATES - WAITING PERIODS

Certain states have waiting periods when you buy on tax sales or foreclosures (Illinois, for example). A person being foreclosed may have two years or so to redeem property, paying you interest for your holding period. You can still participate in buying tax sales or foreclosed properties, but there are two additional things you should do: (1) check your particular state laws for waiting periods before bidding, and (2) be ready to rent property out during the waiting period. That way you can generate thousands of dollars rental income during your wait. If original owner eventually redeems, you have made several thousand dollars in addition to interest he must pay to redeem. If he does not redeem, at end of waiting period you can sell without hesitation for profit. To check state law, contact state real estate commission and buy copy of commissioner's handbook for a few dollars!

Chapter 15

HOW TO BUY PROPERTY EQUITY AT 10¢ ON THE DOLLAR, THREE METHODS TO USE

WHAT ABOUT BROKERS? CAN THEY CUT YOU OUT? UNRECORDED LOAN DANGERS?

For the most part, brokers are little competition on properties in foreclosure. They not only must exact a sizeable commission from the owner who is already in trouble, but properties in foreclosure are frequently run-down, look ratty on the surface, compared with other properties listed by the same broker. Further, the time element is usually such, that often it is difficult for the broker to get a qualified, interested buyer in the decreasing timespan between publication of foreclosure, and the actual foreclosure itself. In every state of the Union, loans are being foreclosed all the time and the collateral (property, houses, acreage) being repossessed. In every state some public NOTICE must be given of the imminent legal action.

What are the disadvantages of dealing direct with the owner being foreclosed, Method #1? The owner may not give you good precise information about the loans recorded on the property. However, if you are interested in a particular property, say half a mile from your house, a property easy to own, manage, and resell, it is a simple matter to check the county recorder's office for all recorded liens and loans. You can also find out name of lender, and try to arrange financing in advance of purchase. Do not worry about unrecorded loans; you can put a clause in the bill of sale that says you are not responsible for any unrecorded liens or unrecorded loans by the owner. At the county recorder's office you can also check how far taxes are in arrears. If you deal direct

with the owner, you will have to make some provision
for dealing with the holders of other loans on the property (e. g. , a 2nd mortgage, 3rd mortgage, 2nd trust
deed, or some other kind of loan). Following chapters,
entitled "Financing the Foreclosure", and "Dealing
With Lenders", tells you how to deal with subordinate
lenders, at 10¢ to 50¢ on the dollar. Your editor is
interested only in properties that are being foreclosed on 1st mortgage or 1st trust deed. (Those
terms are used interchangeable here , although they
do have subtle legal differences.) Why only "first"
loans?

YOU PROFIT BY HELPING OTHER LENDERS -- AT 10¢ ON $$$!

When a property is foreclosed on a 1st loan, it
usually wipes out all other loans, and title passes free
and clear to the 1st lender foreclosing. 2nd loans and
3rd loans, subordinate liens, are WIPED OUT! Therefore, the holders of that subordinate paper (2nd loans,
etc.) can be highly motivated to sell to you for 10¢ on
the dollar. (In the following chapter, the section cap-
tioned "How to Wipe Out Property Liens at a Small
Fraction on the Dollar" explains how to get these people
to agree to sell to you if you acquire the property--so
that you have their signed agreement -- BEFORE PUT-
TING up any money -- until the day of sale, until the
sale on the property goes through! After all, if the
1st lender forecloses, subordinate lenders lose everything. Here you do them a SERVICE by giving them at
least something on their shaky-paper subordinate
loans. By dealing direct with owners being foreclosed, and with other lenders who are going to see
their loans wiped out when the 1st lender forecloses,
you do both the owners substantial service and you
also do the holders of subordinate paper substantial
service -- getting them money (at least some) on what
otherwise would soon become worthless paper!

Remember the time schedule is working in your FAVOR. As the day of trustee sale or foreclosure auction approaches closer and closer, the owner and the subordinate lenders are more and more highly motivated to deal with you. If subordinate lenders will not deal with you at a few cents on the dollar for their paper -- you have no risk -- you can let the property go into foreclosure (that brings you to the 2nd stage in the process of buying foreclosures, the 2nd basic way to buy foreclosures at the trustee auction). What will happen next?

DEALING AT THE TRUSTEE AUCTION - YOUR SECOND OPPORTUNITY TO ACQUIRE FORECLOSED PROPERTY - METHOD #2

Usually there is a trustee for a savings and loan, bank or other lender who will sell the property at public auction, with DULY PUBLISHED NOTICE, on a certain day at a certain time at a certain location. This trustee will open the bidding, qualify the bidders, and arrange payment for the property. Usually the 1st lender, if it is a bank, or savings and loan, (and if it is a decent property) will bid the price of the mortgage (to protect their interest). Example, if a $34,000 conservatively appraised house is being foreclosed on a $23,000 mortgage, the savings and loan will usually bid $23,000. You may bid $23,100 and acquire the $34,000 property! Buying at foreclosure auctions, or trustee sales, is one TERRIFIC WAY to buy. We have purchased properties as low as 35¢ on the conservatively appraised dollar at trustee sales.

What is the disadvantage to trustee sales? The disadvantage is that you frequently have to pay all cash, or cashier's check. This means if that property is being bid at $23,100 you would have to come up with that amount of money, usually right then and there! In some states you may have a couple of days to raise the money, but in others you must have the

cash available. If you _can_ raise the cash* to bid at
trustee sale, it's only one way to get good _clean_
properties _fast_. Then, assuming the property is a
good clean deal, as soon as you have purchased it
you can turn around and _arrange_ a NEW MORTGAGE,
possibly with a different lender, and get your money
out. For example, if you bought that same $34,000
property for $23,100 you would probably have little
difficulty getting a mortgage for at least $20,000 on a
$34,000 property. In fact, occasionally we hear of
cases where people "mortgage out" for more than they
paid for the property. So don't feel that your money
is going to be tied up all the time you own that property.
You should be able to mortgage the property for part,
or sometimes all, of what you paid, if you bought it
right.

Trustee sales are a _great_ way to acquire property.
Your editor has been at trustee auctions, where he and
lender were the only bidders! When the lender bid the
price of the mortgage he just had to go a few dollars
above the price of the 1st mortgage to acquire the
property! There _was_ _no_ competition!

On the other hand, in smaller communities, or
on very highly desirable properties that have been
well publicized, there could be a number of bidders.
Usually, however, competition is _not_ very stiff at
trustee sales. After all, how many people could raise
$23,100 in cash on short notice? That, alone, usually
eliminates much of your potential competition! On
higher-priced properties, requiring larger amounts
of cash, there is usually less competition than on
lower-priced properties (though individual situations
vary greatly).

Suppose you can't acquire the property from the
owner. Also suppose you cannot raise sufficient cash
to bid the price of the mortgage at the trustee sale.
What do you do then?

*See Chapter   , which explains several ways to
raise cash for an impending deal.

112

HIDDEN VALUES IN FORECLOSURE SALES - A LAST CHANCE FOR YOU TO WHEEL AND DEAL - DIRECT! (METHOD #3)

Don't give up hope. You can still <u>deal</u> direct with the foreclosing lender (winning bidder) who will be the new legal owner of the property after the trustee auction. That's right, let's suppose that lender acquires that same property for $23,000, price of the mortgage. You can go to him the day after the auction and say "Mr. Lender, I know you are in the lending business, not the property acquisition business. I'll take that disturbing property off your hands and give you an extra $1500 profit, $24,500. In return I want you to give me a new mortgage on that property at the going rate. You'll have a $1500 profit, Mr. Lender, and you'll have a bad loan off the books, and you'll have a sound good-pay <u>new loan</u> on the property with which you are <u>already</u> familiar. Furthermore, Mr. Lender, I intend to <u>improve</u> that property, repaint it, landscape it, and <u>add value</u> in MANY <u>ways</u>. Therefore, instead of being stuck with a ratty-looking property, on which taxes are accumulating, on which you are earning no interest on the money you have tied up, I can <u>solve</u> all those <u>problems</u> for you, Mr. <u>Lender.</u>"

You should deal with the lender SOON after he acquires a property. If that lender puts in $3000 to $5000 in repairs and cosmetic refinishing on that property, so it can be resold through a broker at a substantial commission, that lender is going to try and get <u>as much as possible</u> for the property. He'll put it on the market at around the $34,000 appraised price. To deal with the lender, you have to deal <u>quick</u>, and fast. Once that lender gets monetarily involved for more than the price of the mortgage, once 6 or 8 brokers go to him (since they know who acquired the property at the foreclosure auction) and try to get him to list that property for full ticket, the lender will be <u>less receptive</u> to your offer. Therefore, get to the lender before others do!

When you offer to buy that property from foreclosing lender you should be able to save at least the
price of the broker's commission (and often substan-
tially more $$$) no matter when you talk to the lender.
After all, if you've been following this property right
through the foreclosure process, to learn your way,
and try to acquire it, you already have an advantage
over the broker who is trying to list the property.
Furthermore, you're a new strong buyer -- and you
came direct to the lender prior to the broker contact-
ing lender. The broker didn't bring you, you brought
yourself before the broker could even appear on the
scene. That gives you an advantage with the lender.

Once you begin acquiring property through loan
defaults or foreclosures, you may never buy a prop-
erty the regular way again! Further, buying proper-
ties in foreclosure can be easily handled on weekends,
or by a person who has another steady job, and not
much time. If you can turn 1 or 2 property deals per
year, you may even make more than at your regular
salary, whatever it is, while you retain your steady
job! Isn't that worth a little bit of perseverance on
your part?

Again, push forward with BULLDOG determina-
tion. Haunt the county recorder's office until you find
out how, when, where those properties are auctioned
in your county on unpaid loans. Find out where the
legal notices are published, where they're posted,
with names and addresses of legal owners. Don't be
discouraged -- don't give up when bureaucrats,
brokers or insiders try to discourage you. After all,
no one is anxious to have you in there as an additional
bidder. Those presently acquiring the properties on
loans in default are not anxious to have you as bidding
competition. County clerks are not always motivated
to educate you. Whether you plan to acquire property
immediately, or later on is immaterial -- you will

114

have learned something, and that's <u>worth</u> <u>money</u> --
BIG MONEY whenever YOUR big deal comes along!
Good luck!

Chapter 16

SETTING UP THE FIRST INTERVIEW

One of the big success secrets in dealing with foreclosures is going to be your personal attitude. If you wish to make thousands of dollars in this area, you are going to have to adopt a certain "problem - solving" attitude and a description of that attitude is appropriate here. Furthermore, the people with whom you will be dealing will be somewhat "strange" and they will also have a certain attitude; hence, a description of their attitude is also appropriate.

Your personal attitude should be orderly, problem-solving, positive and businesslike, not sloppy, disorderly or haphazard. Just consider how long it would take you to work at your present hourly wage to make $5,000 or $10,000, after taxes, and you will see this is worth some precise effort.

The people with whom you will deal have proven their inability to cope with their problems or they wouldn't be in foreclosure. You are going to have to demonstrate your ability to solve their problems and thereby solve your own profit problem in the process. You won't have much competition in this regard because brokers will be taking an entirely different approach.

You will be doing these people a favor, helping them to get thousands of dollars of equity out of their property that they wouldn't get unless you were there. Remember that within a few short weeks, a bank or savings and loan is going to own that property for the price of the mortgage that is on it! Which is better - that the bank or savings and loan own the property for the price of the mortgage? Or that you buy the property, giving a few thousand dollars lost equity to the owner that he would not otherwise receive, and you assume the mortgage? Which is better for the owner? Is he better off having the record of a complete foreclosure buffeting his credit standing for the next few years? Or is the present owner better off selling to you, getting some cash out of the deal and saving his already poor credit from a devastating blow? You can see already where you are in a position to do these people a favor and solve some of their problems.

At first they may not realize what you can do for them. They can't be thinking too clearly or they probably would not be in foreclosure in the first place. Remember that you are going into a problem situation that has existed for many months, long before you appeared on the scene or even knew about it!

You already know a good deal about the people from the "Notice of Default" source. Approach them during daylight hours only. People who have problems might give you a bad reception at any other time. Don't come on like gangbusters, driving up in a fancy new car and a $300 suit. Someone who looks like the people they know will get a friendlier reception. Let them know at the door that you are interested in buying their house. The next point is very important. They will immediately ask how you heard about it -- because many of them never mention selling to anyone. It is at this point that you drop the bomb. You let them know you saw a public notice of their property going into foreclosure! This brings them to a sense of reality. Tell them you might be able to help them. Exchange names and telephone numbers and let them know what time they can reach you (example, after 6 p.m., weekends only, etc.)

You are conducting this in a business-like manner now, so as to make certain that you can be reached at a certain time at a certain place every week. If they offer to show you the premises, fine. Look them over. If not, leave immediately. Many will say they have no intention of selling, but make sure they get your name, phone number and time available anyway - since they are going to be out of there in a few weeks whether they have such "intentions" or not.

After the first interview, time is on your side. You are not going to buy this place in one interview. The first stage, the initial approach, serves only as introduction, exposing the owner to the "problem-solving" cash-available attitude.

The second stage is where they call you. That is much more simple and business-like. Their thinking is already improving. They are coming back to reality. You are the person with some chance to solve their problem, a chance to help them, in a situation that is deteriorating (for them). Within 90 days that property is going to be advertised for sale by the bank or mortgage holder. Period.

It is during the second stage that you tell them precisely what you could do for them -- (a) coming up with some money for them, (b) saving their credit, (c) protecting them from a deficiency judgment on the property, and (d) for someone who is looking for an out from a deplorable situation, you can also help them achieve that goal faster.

During this second stage you also try to get them to set their rock-bottom price. You will only get to the second stage with a percentage of the people you approach, so it is important to keep moving. Get some volume, making approaches to 50 properties to assure 10 will call you back for the second stage. The time you spend today, the hours of effort you make, are your thousand-dollar bills of tomorrow. Don't make one first-stage approach and then stop. Generate volume. Keep moving.

Chapter 17

APPRAISING THE HOUSE

When you are invited back to a house, you need a notebook, a steno pad, and a good map. Prior to the first stage you should have set up a little chart for yourself, containing the time you first approached them, name, address, general appearance of neighborhood, etc. On the same chart, during the second stage, you will note the problem if they want to tell you about it. You will also evaluate nearby properties. If there are any brokers or "for sale" signs on properties down the street, you make some phone calls to find what similar houses are listed at.

Once inside the house, on friendlier terms than the first visit, look around. Any house that has payments missed for four or five months has not been maintained for a year or more. That means all these houses need work. That's why you will have little competition from brokers. Not only will brokers be trying to sell these houses at full ticket plus their 6% commission, the brokers will also be showing houses without problems. Ninety percent of the time a potential buyer does not want a house with problems. Foreclosures always have problems.

Why doesn't the owner just fix it up and sell it easier? If the owner had the money to maintain and bring the house up to salable condition, chances are it would not be in foreclosure in the first place! The present owner has been in financial difficulty for many months, maybe one to three years before you ever met him.

Some day you are going to be faced with reselling this house. What can you pay for it? For easy figuring, let us assume this is a $30,000 tract house with

119

a $17,000 mortgage. When the time comes to resell this house, in order to move it quickly, you want to sell at least 10% under market. If similar houses in the same area are for sale at $30,000, deduct 10%, or $3,000, immediately. Also, deduct 6% brokerage commission. Since you are going to do much of the broker's work yourself, you might as well make the commission. Knock another $1,800 off the price. Deduct $1,000 for hidden maintenance problems that you can't see quickly, and figure in your notebook what else has to be replaced. Let's assume for the sake of an example, that you see another $700 worth of work. (You will be amazed at your ability to appraise and estimate these figures after going through a few houses.)

Don't criticize the property to the owner's face. After all, you are a guest. When making notes throughout the house, wonder out loud, "I wonder if these drapes will have to be replaced? I wonder if the carpet will have to be replaced, with these six bare spots?", etc. You are performing a function here, a very important one. You are getting an unrealistic person to think realistically, as you go through your inspection and appraisal. The guy will be wasting your time if he thinks he is going to get full ticket for a poorly maintained, distressed property. Most owners will respect you for being smart enough to buy a house this way! Some will even tell you they wish they had bought it this way. You can tell them, in a pleasing manner, what fine plans you have to fix it up.

You have now deducted most of the expenses that you are going to incur on the house. Don't forget to deduct $600 or so as "loan assumption" costs which you are going to have to pay the present lender in order for you to take over the present financing. There are also going to be payments, taxes and insurance that have to be brought up to date. These amounts can easily be ferreted out from the lender. Don't worry about them here. You are dealing now with the present owner. Furthermore, you are here to make a profit. You are not making all this effort and doing all this work for your health. On a $30,000 piece of real estate, a 10% profit is quite in order and very conservative. Deduct another $3,000 for your potential profit. Also deduct 3% for "margin of error."

After all these deductions you know approximately how much you can go tops for this place. (The following pages contain a form which may help you with these deductions.) At this point, do not reveal your figure to the owner. You get the owner to tell you, in a friendly way, what his rockbottom value is. It is very important that you get a price. "Come on, Mr. Smith, tell me your very best price right now if I were to buy this house from you today." Let us say he gives you a figure of $25,000. You know you can pay tops of $19,000.

At this point you leave and make certain he has your name and phone number. Chances are pretty good at this point that you will get a call from him a few days or weeks later, nearer and nearer the fore-closure deadline. At that point you can tell him what your top dollar is.

HISTORY SHEET

Date Of Default Action _____ District _____

Address _____

Owners Name _____

Telephone Number _____

Beneficiary 1st Loan _____

                     Amount Owing

                     Monthly Payments

        _____   _____

2nd Loan _____

                     Amount Owing

                     Monthly Payments

        _____   _____

3rd Loan _____

                     Amount Owing

                     Monthly Payments

        _____   _____

Total Number of Payments Delinquent _____

Plus Delinquent Charges   _____

Taxes Delinquent   _____

Taxes Impounded? _____ Amount   _____

Fire Insurance   _____

            Total Delinquency _____

Approx. Escrow and Title Company Charges _____

Assumption Charge   _____

Misc. Charge   _____

Total (estimated) Refurbishing Cost   _____

   Grand Total Initial & Capital Outlay   _____

   Plus whatever money you give to owner   _____

Current Market Value of Property _____ _____

Minus Cushion —   _____

Minus Profit Margin —   _____

Minus Refurbishing Cost →   _____

Total, Assumption Charges —   _____

                                     Total

Minus Refurbishing Cushion   _____ _____

   Net Pay-Out Price _____

Taxes _____ Square Footage _____

Size of Lot _____ No. of Bedrooms _____

No. of Bathrooms _____ Swimming Pool _____ (Filter)

Garage _____ Corner Lot _____ Inside Lot _____

General Appearance of House _____

_____

Needs Paint _____ Inside _____ Outside _____

What Other Decorating Necessary _____

_____

Kitchen _____ (check *ALL* electric equipment such as
  disposals — *Dish-washer* — heating units — air conditioning

Roof _____

Landscaping _____ Sprinkler System___ _____

Bathrooms _____ Showers_____ Toilet_____
  (try showers — flush toilets)

IMPORTANT — Check Inside Toilet Flushing Unit For Date
  Which House Was Built. Also, Check *Electric Meter* For Date

Condition Of All Glass _____

Is Home Close To Schools _____ Shopping _____

Freeway _____ Is Neighborhood Clean and

Well Landscaped _____ Are There Any Parks _____

Is The Street Dedicated _____ Un-Dedicated _____

Remarks —

Date Of 1st Call _____ 2nd Call _____

3rd Call _____ 4th Call _____

Connected To Sewer _____ _____ Septic Tank _____

Chapter 18

FINANCING THE FORECLOSURE

Your goal, to finish the foreclosure purchase, is to roll over the existing financing. Your goal is to let the present paper "ride" on the property rather than getting expensive new loans. Furthermore, you wish to get interest rates on these existing loans knocked down to less than the going present rate. How do you do it?

Perhaps first, to properly motivate you, you should consider what enormous savings are possible. On a $40,000, 20-year mortgage, a mere $1\frac{1}{2}$% difference in interest rate could mean many thousands of dollars: $1\frac{1}{2}$% of $40,000 is only $600 per year. But consider that amount compounded and being added to each and every year as long as you own the property! Even if you own the property only a few years, or transfer the property at an existing low interest rate to a new buyer, the advantages are tremendous. Savings are enormous, particularly if you get three to six of these properties going for you at the same time!

How do you get better interest rates than others? Let's assume you have checked 60 properties, interviewed approximately 20 out of those 60 in which you were interested, and five of those 20 called you back. Let us assume you are now ready to work on a $30,000 market value property with a $17,000 first mortgage. Your goal is to get into that property for a maximum of $2,000 and pick up an additional $10,000 potential profit for yourself, rolling over the existing mortgage. (The terms "mortgage" and "trust deed" are used interchangeably.)

Recognize you are in a <u>contest</u>, a <u>struggle</u>. It is a psychological wrestling match. There are <u>roles</u> that must be played in this wrestling match, both by you and the lending officer. You are both going to repeat things in each other's presence that are <u>obvious</u>, but they must be repeated anyway. For psychological reasons in this match, it must be clear to the lending officer who <u>he</u> is. You summarize briefly: it is he who has the responsibility of lending depositors' money in safety, depositors in his financial institution. <u>He</u> has the problem! The guy being foreclosed has the problem! <u>You</u> <u>don't</u> <u>have</u> the <u>problem</u> (at least not until you put up some of your own money!).

It must be clear at the outset of this match that you are a <u>problem solver</u>, and that you are willing to undertake the lending officer's problem and the owner's problem, but <u>only</u> under certain <u>specific conditions</u>. When the negotiations get moving, repeat to yourself frequently, "I am a problem solver." This will help keep the negotiations on the proper track and keep identities clearly segregated. In the role-playing game, the lending officer will rattle off certain terms and conditions he is interested in. That is how he identifies himself. <u>Don't interrupt</u> him. Let him get it off his chest. It is only after he has said his piece (and spent some of his strength, to your satisfaction) that negotiations begin in earnest.

This problem of identity is very important psychologically in getting low interest rates. You must identify yourself to the lending officer, not only by name, but as a speculator. Learn the terminology. You aren't talking about properties -- but REO's. REO is a word that strikes fear to the heart of any lending officer. A growing list of REO's causes boards of directors of financial institutions to quake with fear. The number of REO's is a yardstick, a measurement, by which the performance of a lending institution is often evaluated. So are delinquent loans.

As you chat with the lending officer, let him know that you are "interested in taking over the problem on spec" (speculation). Put it just that way. You are not interested in buying that property. The lending officer will respect you for identifying yourself in this manner and treat you in a far different manner than he would an ordinary borrower. This is one way you change the rules in your favor.

Another important characteristic of the proper attitude is that of "interested indifference." Psychologically, it is very difficult to be interested but indifferent after you have looked at 60 properties and conducted 20 interviews to get to this one. However, you <u>must</u> <u>discipline</u> yourself to be "interested but indifferent." It pays off! BIG!

Perhaps an illustration will clarify. Maybe some of you have traveled in the West Appalachian hill country and some of the Appalachian communities. If you go to a small town where you are a stranger and have a difficult transaction to get through in a hurry, what happens when you try to force it? If you put the pressure on those country people you will wait till doomsday to get your important business done. They will take every little problem of every one of their friends first, ahead of yours. On the other hand, if you go into that same situation with an attitude of "interested indifference," chances are they will work hard to get your business completed first. Push them, and they back away. Give them a friendly break, and they will go to work for you.

INCREASING THE STAKE

During the initial loan interview, you must let the loan officer know you are mildly interested in getting such-and-such done, but only if it is going to be done in a certain specific manner by a certain specific time. You let him know you realize the matter is totally in their hands.

This attitude of "interested indifference" is in direct contrast to the attitude with which most people march in to make a loan. Most folks go in with a "hat-in-hand," somewhat desperate, often tense outlook. It is the surest way to kill a good loan deal.

In this little match you must assert every bit of leverage at your command, but in an easy-going manner. You start stacking up the chips in front of the loan officer psychologically, so that he can't afford not to negotiate the best possible deal. First of all, if you are in a medium-size or small town, and you have known these people in the past, draw on your past relationship. Play it up. Another chip into the pot. Second, you might casually let it slip that, if the loan committees were willing to grant you an interest rate one-quarter or one-half a point below anyone else, you might be willing to deposit a few thousand dollars extra into the lending institution. Nothing in writing -- just another chip thrown into the pot.

Third, if you are going to be a professional speculator, buy yourself a $20 Polaroid camera and casually flip one or two photos of the distressed property on the lending officer's desk. "You can keep these for your file, Mr. Loan Officer, whether I assume the existing loan or not. They give you an idea of what shape your foreclosure is in. See the broken window, peeling paint, etc." This time you threw a handful of psychological chips into the pot, increasing the stakes.

Now for your sideways attack. Mention a name. It can be the name of anyone the loan officer already knows. It might be the teller who directed you to the loan officer. It might be another depositor who does business at the lending institution. It might be someone else who sits on the loan committee. It might be the name of a lending officer at another institution. It doesn't matter very much how well the loan officer knows the name you mention, as long as he knows it.

He must be made psychologically aware that there is likely to be third-party interest in your progress on this loan negotiation. Loan officers, like other middle-management people, sometimes have a vague insecurity. They don't want any third party coming to them later and asking, "Why did you turn down Mr. Jones, my friend?" With this "flank" attack, you have thrown some more psychological chips into the pot. You can add more as they are available to you. The important thing is to make the stake so high that this lending officer cannot afford to give you anything but the very best rate on the loan.

You must have a prosperous look. Lending officers like to loan money to the people who look like they don't need money. If you look like you need the money, forget it. No matter what your occupation, look sharp. Even if you are an 18-year-old student, you will be respected and treated as a professional speculator if you look the part.

At this point, all that remains to be done is nail down the actual interest rate. Loan officers, when given the opportunity, will duck behind the saying "The loan committee decides on that" (even though the loan officer is probably on that three-man committee, and invariably it follows his personal recommendation). Always ask the lending officer what his lowest interest rate for prime properties with highest down payments is, (even though you may only intend to put 10% down). Get that figure early in the interview, not later. Don't talk about what their common practice is on risky loans -- only on prime loans.

Here's another chip. If the prime rate has come down recently, mention it. If the lending institution is now paying a lower rate on savings deposits, mention it. Not only are you trying to get lower interest rates; you are also trying to raise barriers against a jump in the interest rate after you leave. The purpose of mentioning the obvious is both to get lower interest rates and also to prevent a later jump before the final papers are signed.

At this point get a proposed commitment, verbally, from the loan officer. Don't ask him to put it in writing. Chances are the loan committee is going to go along 90% of the time with whatever the loan officer's recommendation is anyway.

Chapter 19

DEALING WITH OTHER LENDERS --
HOW TO WIPE OUT PROPERTY LIENS
AT A SMALL FRACTION ON THE DOLLAR

Sometimes a foreclosure property may have a second mortgage and even a third mortgage.

If the lender holding the first mortgage is foreclosing, the second mortgage holder may be cut out without getting a penny!

If you want to take over that first mortgage by dealing with the property owner before foreclosure, must you pay second mortgage in full, too?

No! Here's how to get rid of that second or third mortgage at 10¢ to 40¢ on the dollar! Go directly to whomever holds the second mortgage. Usually it's a private investor (a doctor, a dentist, a previous owner, the guy's brother-in-law, etc.). Tell the second mortgage holder he stands to lose everything if the first mortgage holder forecloses. Offer him 10¢ to 25¢ on the dollar for the second mortgage. For example, if the second mortgage is $2500, offer him $250 to $600 for his interest in the property. At first he may be shocked; shocked to even discover "his property" going into foreclosure! Later on, as foreclosure day approaches, chances are he will sell you that second mortgage at 25¢ on the dollar or less. Be reluctant -- until you get your price! This is a very easy way to make thousands of extra dollars on a property.

IMPORTANT: Do not pay any money to the second mortgage holder until you have the signed "option to buy" agreement from the property owner. Don't risk your dollars on the first or second mortgage until you have that property tied down.

Coordination is the key. Let the risk remain theirs until everyone has agreed to your offers and terms. Get a signed agreement from each -- but don't lay your money on the line until you are personally satisfied. This is how to buy second and third mortgages at a discount on your properties.

WHAT'S NEEDED FOR YOU TO START MAKING $$$

Admittedly, the psychological techniques and pressures outlined for your use and for your own benefit here, are unusual. If they seem dramatic, so is the stake. For 15 to 20 minutes of well-disciplined performance on your part, you may save a minimum of $500 to many thousands of dollars on your next real estate loan. In fact, many of you will improve on the basic techniques outlined here and add your own "chips." Whatever the unusual effort required, the per-hour "pay" is well worth it!

These techniques will work even when you are dealing with unforeclosed properties. For example, income properties are sold at a multiple of net yearly earnings. Interest rate expense comes right off the top of earnings. Therefore, if you can lower interest rate expense you can increase net earnings on income properties. If you can increase net earnings on the income property, you can create an accelerated multiplier effect on the sale price of that property, thereby setting yourself up for a gigantic capital gain!

You need several things to succeed in foreclosures. You need $2,000 to $5,000 minimum capital, and a willingness to learn. If you are serious about this, you can make more money than at your present job. It is a wonderful hobby for young people and people who are retired, people with more time than money. It is something that couples or individuals can handle very nicely on weekends.

Chapter 20

WORKING PERSON'S FAMILY
FIVE-PRONG HOUSING STRATEGY

Housing expense accounts for 25% to 33% of the average person's after-tax earnings (take home pay). Housing expense will account for roughly 20% of the average worker's pre-tax earnings.

That means that housing is the biggest drain from the wage earner's family budget. Surprisingly enough, it is seldom looked upon as a "drain" by those in rental units. The homeowner is usually aware of the extent of the cash drain, but not so with many who are renting.

As inflation moves EVERYONE into higher and higher tax brackets, SHELTER expense (or housing expense, if you prefer) will assume even more importance. Therefore, it is in your best interest, if you earn $6,000 or more per year, to look to cutting the outflow and increasing the inflow, making money if possible, from the shelter money-drain.

Continued inflation means everyone will be carried into the higher tax brackets. Government will take a larger and larger portion of our earnings, not only for rising social security benefits, already legislated, but will also take a bigger percentage of your regular taxed wage and income earnings. We know, with reasonable certainty from Kamin's law and other economic observations, that inflation is likely to increase and prices continue their upward spiral over at least the next 1-2 years.

Therefore, with these assumptions, your strategy is appropriate to get as much tax write-off as possible, since you have to shelter yourself and your family anyway. Take care of the biggest

take-home "payshrinker" and get yourself the same
bit of tax shelter that millionaires have found essential. Too many times we meet young folks just out of
school or service who are doomed to 10 years or 15
years of NO TAX SHELTER because "Renting is so
much easier," "I don't know anything about real estate," "I haven't got the money," "I don't want to be
tied down," and innumerable other excuses. Get
smart!

    1. Interest on mortgage is a tax write-off.
Whether your tax bracket is 15% or 30%, or 50%, get
every tax write-off you can. On a $30,000 mortgage
at 9% interest, that is $2,700 of tax write-off per
year! If you are in a 25% tax bracket (state and federal combined) that is $675 cash money you are
throwing away by renting.

    2. Property taxes are a legitimate tax write-
off too. A $1,000 property tax in a 30% (combined
state and federal income tax bracket means $300 cash
in your pocket if you get the write-off. There are
other deductions for owning a home that are also tax
write-offs, but these are two big ones. Under certain conditions, you can take a depreciation deduction,
you can deduct expenses of an office at home where
required by your business, and even sometimes allo-
cate maintenance expenses as such for legit deductions
(including electricity, gas heating). I further suggest
that you don't do your own income tax. Usually $25
to $100 per year will get a professional job done and
give you an opportunity to verify accuracy, making
sure you don't miss legitimate deductions.

    "Ah," says the renter, "I don't have to pay all
that property tax and mortgage interest and maintenance and so on - I just pay my rent." Not so, taxes,
mortgage interest, maintenance and other expenses
go to MAKE UP your RENT, or the biggest portion of
it.   Therefore, you are paying, even third hand,
property taxes, mortgage interest, whether you know

it or not - whether you get the tax deduction as owner or not. If you are going to pay it, you might as well structure your affairs so you get the same bit of tax shelter as the millionaires, even as our president does.

3. As you get the tax benefits of improved property ownership, you should double the fun by trying to MAKE SOME MONEY out of it. Inflation will inexorably move you into a higher tax bracket. Don't believe us? Were you aware that the income tax was started out as a temporary 1% levy? Look at your bracket today! Therefore, your strategy should be to shoot for long-term capital gains to MAKE MONEY in CHUNKS, not income alone from wages and salary. It should be the thinking goal of every wage earner to make additional amounts on a capital gains basis at the earliest possible date. That is the only way you can CUT your TAX BITE on ordinary income by half. This strategy means that you will shoot to win huge PROFITS from whatever dwelling you buy TO HOUSE YOUR FAMILY, and also on any OTHER PROPERTY you might buy. When you are a renter, your first and primary goal ought to be to get all the tax shelter possible from housing your family. Your second and more sophisticated goal should be to make a huge chunk of money on whatever dwelling you buy. Surprisingly enough, homeowners are often astounded to discover how their dwelling increases in value over a period of time! Summarily, tax shelter is an intermediate goal, but making a chunk of profit is the big goal. There is no reason you can't DO BOTH TOGETHER instead of being just dependent on a job for your total income. If history is any guide, inflation is going to hit hardest at the wage earner.

4. Keep your eye on the ball. DON'T GET INVOLVED in property JUST FOR the INCOME the rentals may provide. Your goal when buying an income property is to RAISE RENTS AS QUICKLY as

possible so that you can RAISE the SALE PRICE.
Sale price is often a multiple of income generated by
the property.

5. You make your money NOT from collecting
rents but from IMPROVING the property and selling
it for a much HIGHER price. Your real income is
the difference between what you paid and what you
sold it for, a capital gain; don't become mesmerized
by rental income. Keep your eye on the capital gains
ball. Your PROFIT is your REWARD for making a
stagnant property into a sharp improved property
that benefits the new OWNER and the TENANTS alike,
as well as benefitting all the NEIGHBORS.

HOW TO LOWER THE RISK WHEN BUYING PROPERTY!

Even if you know little or nothing about real estate, there are three ways to help lower risk, even
on your first purchase. Naturally, you have to "step
out of your rut," and begin to do your homework in
your area.

1. The first way to lower risk is to buy distressed property way BELOW conservative AP-
PRAISALS, below market. Brokers and relatives
will tell you it can't be done, your friends will tell
you "it's crazy," but they are mistaken, it CAN be
done and is being done right now!

2. Once you have acquired a distressed property, you further lower the risk by refinancing, by
upping the mortgage. It is almost always wise to
borrow as much as possible at the lowest possible interest rate to get all the money out of the property as
fast as possible. Example: You buy a $20,000 ram-
shackle house at a county probate sale for $11,000.
The tax assessor has appraised that house at $19,000.
You borrowed from Aunt Minnie to get the cash to do
it, or made a deal with your friendly banker. Now
you rework the property as described in this book.

135

Use it or rent it out for $350 a month, and re-
mortgage the property that is now worth $25,000
(since you put lots of time, money and work in it) for
$20,000. Now you have $20,000 on a $25,000 proper-
ty, Aunt Minnie has been repaid, and you either have
rental income or shelter for your family to help with
the new higher mortgage payments.

    3. You have $9,000 extra to play with to do it
again on a bigger property. Until you sell that property, you can use these $9,000 in revenues, tax free.
Note how you have also lowered your risk with this
purchase.

        a. You bought way below market, so that
even if you made a mistake, it won't be too costly.
You got in cheap enough to allow for your beginning
mistakes. Don't be afraid of mistakes.

        b. You got your original stake back out, and
passed the risk to the lender, the mortgage holder.
He now assumes 80% of the risk on that property (a
$20,000 mortgage on a $25,000 improved dwelling).
But note how, by improving that property, you made
his loan MORE SECURE. If you should default, he
probably would have a much easier time disposing of
that property. He doesn't have to sink money into a
disgusting probate lending deal. He got a nice
salable property, even if you, as buyer, should default. You got your stake out plus some additional
revenues to improve the property and your use for
other helpful deals again. You lowered the risk for
yourself, for the lenders - and improved things for
the heirs or the Probate Court by bidding higher for
that house than the other bidders present. That
meant that the heirs got more money. YOU HELPED
EVERYONE and the profit, when you go to sell, is
your reward.

        c. Now you can resell for profit and do it
again. Every time you make a sizable real estate
capital gains profit, you become better financed,

improve new deals, reduce risk on future deals. There is no reason why you can't make an extra year's income each one or two years, given the will and a little capital to try!

Now let us mention one thing you will not find in any of the real estate textbooks or college courses or commissioners' handbooks or brokers' manuals: "THERE IS LESS RISK AT DEALING IN DISTRESSED PROPERTY IN THE MANNER DESCRIBED THAN THERE IS IN ORDINARY NEW HOUSING OR ORDINARY CONDOMINIUM PURCHASES!" If you lower risk, follow the three steps above and make an extra year or two capital gain income for each year or two you work. Make it in a capital gains CHUNK that is TAXED at a LOWER rate.

Chapter 21

SELLING YOUR PROPERTY - SAVE COMMISSIONS

Don't become so enthusiastic about speculating in real estate that you overlook "How to Sell" your property. The most important part of this speculating business is the buying. However, selling is a very important part of the equation, and unless you have at least average competence in sales, you will find it difficult to get your money out.

PREPARE FOR THE SALE

WAYS TO UP YOUR PROFIT

When you are ready to sell your property, it must look good. That means "cosmetic" finishing. It means freshly-cut lawns, fresh paint, hosed and washed sidewalks and other facilities.

It is impossible to keep a residence in dewy fresh condition all the time; therefore, you must schedule your selling efforts for a particular week or period of time. You don't place continual advertisements or hold continual open house. Use saturation exposures only during the scheduled period.

Did you ever walk into a new model home? It is not unusual for it to have $18,000 worth of furniture and expensive interior decoration. The poor soul who buys that new home is often shocked to discover ugly, bare, plastered walls and scruffy mounds of dirt in place of the fancy furnishings and landscaping.

Steal a page from the tract-builders book. We know one man who owns over $10,000 worth of furnishings. He moves them into his new speculation, sells the property, and moves them on to the next one.

Most new home buyers make one unwarranted assumption. They walk into a place and assume that it will look as good or better with their own furnishings as it does with the present furniture. Our friend with his $10,000 "moveable showcase" furniture capitalizes on the foolish home buyer's assumption. If you hope to make it easy for yourself to sell properties, you should consider accumulating your own moveable showcase. Your objective will be class. Better one piece far above the average than six pieces of everyday furnishings. Get the very finest "showcase" pieces you can find -- one at a time -- but don't pay full ticket retail.

Buy your moveable showcase at auctions, bankruptcies, warehouse closeouts, estate or divorce sales. It does not matter if the pieces are slightly used, as long as they have class. Remember, they are supposed to look "lived in." Concentrate on a specific period for maximum effect. Examples: French Provincial, or Italian Renaissance. Do it piece by piece with striking pieces only -- no common furnishings.

For striking fixtures, look for a wrecker tearing down an old hotel or apartment house. A $10 bill to the right "hard hat" might get you a chandelier that cost a thousand dollars or a theater rug that cost $30 a yard. If you can't find the buildings being torn down, check the wrecking yard headquarters. They save the best stuff for themselves. Find out where the crews are working from the headquarters.

Anything that is not permanently affixed to the property for sale does not go with the property (planters, fountains, statuaries, patio furniture.) The seller can take it with him. You can buy 25-foot trees in planters that go with you. Use them.

With your moveable showcase, it will help if you can get an interior decorator to put it together in an attractive way. How do you get free talent? Call your local university. Find out the names of the instructors teaching advanced courses in interior decoration. Call those instructors and get the names of their most

talented students. Tell them you will give them a
chance to try their hand with your money and your
high-price showcase furnishings. Tell them you will
pay for all painting, plastering, and other expenses.
You will be astounded, enchanted, and amazed with
what a talented student can do with the old wreck of a
house you bought!

Use students to help you sell during the scheduled
period. When your face-lifted property is ready to be
shown, don't be there! Hire an attractive co-ed, preferably an interior decorator, to be the hostess. Have
a descriptive sheet typed up describing the property.
List your neighbor's property on that sheet, too.
Wherever you see a brokerage sign in the neighborhood, list the price and address on your descriptive
sheet so a prospect looking at your home can compare
and discover what a fabulous buy it is. Offer your
co-ed a nominal daily wage for hosting the open house
plus a big bonus on each completion of sale.

As your hostess shows people the property during
your open house, instruct her not to discuss price or
terms. Tell her to smile nicely and say, "I am sure
Mr. _____ can work something out with you." Your
price and some terms may be listed on the descriptive
sheet you had printed in advance, which your hostess
is passing out to the prospect. Instruct your hostess
to take their name and phone number and to have the
prospects call you for an appointment the day after
they look at the house or as soon as possible thereafter. Get them to your home or your office for
negotiation or meet them at your property.

As prospects inspect your property the second
time they will see all sorts of wonderful things they
would like included with the purchase. They will ask
you questions like, "Are the draperies included?"
"Is the carpeting included?" "Are the washer and
dryer included?" "Are the X, Y, and Z included?"
Your answer is always the same: "No, but I'll make

you a great deal on them." Even if you bought the house with those $300 drapes included, when Mr. Prospect asks if they are included, you tell him no, but that you will make him a good deal on them - for $50. Same way on the carpet. Even though you got that $500 carpeting for nothing when you bought the property, you offer it to the new prospect for $120. In many cases you can squeeze an extra four-figure profit out of the property in this manner and make the prospect happy because he is buying at one-fourth of what it would cost him to install new items! Always make the price tantalizingly low. Maximize profits by not including anything. After all, you do have a bargain price on the property, don't you? And the prospect is saving the broker's commission, isn't he?

HELP THE BUYER WITH FINANCING:

RAISE CASH 3 WAYS

Let's say, for example, you have a property priced at $28,500, with a $19,000 mortgage. The buyer knows the house is a bargain because he has checked the other addresses listed on your descriptive sheet and seen similar houses selling for $31,000 to $35,000. You not only have your property priced attractively, but you have lowered the price $1,500 because you are selling it yourself and saving the broker's commission. That alone enables you to lower the price from $30,000 to $28,500. The prospect realizes he is the beneficiary and is anxious to work something out with you.

Check the down payment required. The difference between your $28,500 price and the $19,000 mortgage is $9,500. That is quite a chunk of cash for a new buyer to come up with, particularly young couples. They will be lucky to have $3,000 to $4,000 in cash.

To solve this problem, there are several sources of cash to check. The first is the banker who has the mortgage. Is he willing to raise that mortgage from $19,000 to, say, $24,000? Find out.

A second source of ready cash is the buyer's own friends, relatives and employer. Everyone has an "Aunt Minnie" who has a few thousand stashed away. The only thing you have to do is motivate the buyer to break down his resistance in asking Aunt Minnie for the money. In many cases, if the buyer works for a small firm, he can borrow cash from his employer. If he works for a large firm, he can probably borrow secured or unsecured cash from the employee credit union. Encourage the buyer to dream up his own way of getting the cash. Most buyers don't even realize they have sources of cash beyond their own limited savings. It will be up to you to educate and encourage your prospect, especially the younger buyers. You must first make them enthusiastic, however, about the property and what a great bargain it is, to make them willing to ask friends, relatives, or employers for the money.

There is a third alternative for fast cash. Most states have small loan companies who will loan a reliable employed person $3,000 to $5,000 without security. If all other sources of sufficient cash fail, march your buyer to Ye Friendly Finance Company before he takes on the house loan. Before he has a big mortgage payment, the finance company may well be willing to cough up a couple thousand dollars which Mr. Prospect can hand to you as part of his down payment. Don't try this after the prospect has applied for a bank loan, as the finance companies now see a change in the picture of the buyer's monthly income and liabilities. (In other words, get the buyer to the finance company while he looks strong, not after he uses up all his savings in making up your down payment.)

One or more of these three alternatives will usually generate sufficient cash for you to get out your entire equity in cash.

Do not take back second trust deeds or second mortgages. Repeat: no second loans. You borrow money via second loans when you buy a property; you don't give them when you sell a property. Be unwilling to carry back paper on sales. Whatever you do, don't take back long-term paper when you make a sale. It is the poorest possible strategy in a period of increasing inflation.

Chapter 22

WHY NEVER TO "TAKE BACK A SECOND" WHEN YOU SELL - WHY NOT TO BUY SECOND TRUST DEEDS, OR SECOND MORTGAGES

Many people who buy second trust deeds for income, for the first time, do not realize that their piece of paper can be made worthless by the first mortgage foreclosure. The second paper holder can be cut out of the picture completely if the first lender forecloses!

One real estate broker we knew bought a house in an area going commercial and loaded it up with first, second and third loans. He got over-extended and did something quite unusual. He kept making the small payments on the second loan and the third loan, but stopped making payments on the first loan! What was the effect? The poor holder of the second loan paper had to come up with the money to pay the first loan! Why? Well, if the first lender foreclosed, the second lender would lose the value of his loan completely. Therefore, second lender had to cough up payments for the first mortgage, while the over-extended owner continued to live in the house rent-free, merely by making the small payments on the second loan and the third loan. Brilliant? Perhaps questionable ethics, but it could happen. Why didn't the second mortgage holder foreclose? He couldn't foreclose! - The payments on the second loan, small though they were, were always paid! Therefore, second lender could not foreclose, but was in danger of being foreclosed himself! Don't ever take second mortgages, buy second mortgages, or second trust deeds. Same way when selling property. Don't take back second mortgages, or second trust deeds.

Help the buyer arrange his own financing. Protection
of your capital is more important than the crummy
6% - 11% interest you might earn.

HOW TO GET RID OF AN EXISTING SECOND
TRUST DEED OR SECOND MORTGAGE!*

Many times a client will come to your author and
say, "Hey, I've got this 2nd trust deed (2nd mortgage)
paying 6% on a property or business I sold 5 years
ago -- what do I do with it? Interest rates are higher
now, and 2nd trust (2nd TD) is not due for another 6
years!" Apparently, many clients were talked into
taking 2nd trust deeds by real estate brokers. This
is favorite tactic of RE brokers, who have a buyer
that can't come up with much cash; the broker wants
the deal badly, so he can get his commission. Of
course, later, the seller is stuck with 2nd TD, a very
difficult item to get rid of. Usually property-seller
is not aware of how tough it may be to dispose of 2nd,
at any reasonable price, until he tries.

Firm principle on 2nd TDs: When you sell property, you take cash. When you buy property, you give
the 2nd trust deed; don't get it backwards.

To put it another way, when you buy property,
you want to give the seller a 2nd TD. Why? (1) If
seller has misled you in any way on the property, 2nd
TD lowers your risk. (2) You can sometimes go back
to property seller a month or more after the transaction is concluded and buy that 2nd TD at a substantial discount (e. g. , buying a $10, 000 face-value 8%
2nd TD for $8, 500). When you sell property, don't
take 2nd TD, regardless of what broker says. Having
fixed-interest return on an unsalable 2nd TD is probably the worst position you can be in, in an inflationary
recession. (A) You don't have use of funds, only piece

*2nd TDs are used in Western U. S. ;
2nd mortgages in Eastern U. S.

145

of paper; (B) You have only a fixed return, of usually 6% - 8%, when prices could rise at 15% per year clip. You would have been better off to keep property.

Okay, so you ignored that advice, or didn't know, didn't realize at the time how difficult it would be to get rid of 2nd TD. Now you're a couple of years down the road, smarter; you need the cash, and 2nd TD doesn't mature for years. What do you do?

Best way to get rid of a 2nd TD is First, don't take any, as pointed out above. Second best way is go to the guy who owes you the money! Tell him, "Mr. Borrower, I know you owe me $10,000 at 6% on the 2nd TD due in 1980. I will make you an offer good for 30 days. If you will buy back that 2nd TD within the next 30 days, I will give you $1,000 discount from face-value. In other words, you can buy back your own IOU, Mr. Borrower, at 90¢ on the dollar."

There is important reason for going back to guy who bought your property. If he was smart enough to give you 2nd TD, and talk you into it, or the broker was, chances are he may jump at chance to buy back his own IOU at discount. Also, his personal cash situation may have changed since he bought your property. Perhaps he has already sold it, for profit, or increased rental income on the property. Perhaps he now has greater borrowing power than when he bought that property. Don't assume that just because he was unable to come up with cash at the time of purchase, he is still unable to come up with the additional cash. A substantial 4-figure discount from the face-value of the 2nd TD that he has to pay in full anyway might just entice him to "cash you out."

Remember, too, this is NEGOTIATING situation. If 10% discount won't entice him, try 20% discount, but put on time limit. You don't want him coming to you a year or two from now or on the day the 2nd TD is due in full, saying, "Okay, I'm here to buy it at a discount!" No; either he has to buy it at a discount

within definite short time, or _lose_ his _chance._ In
this way you convince him to _act_ quickly _or forget_ it.
If there is no time limit, he may not be motivated to
raise fast cash for you. If he asks why you need the
cash, tell him you have unique opportunity soon gone,
and that's why you offer discount. _No need_ to _explain_
further. Suppose the guy really cannot come up with
cash in reasonable period of time?

Third way to get rid of 2nd TD is to arrange
alternate source of _financing_ for the buyer. Example:
You sold a $35,000 house for $20,000 1st mortgage,
$10,000 2nd loan, and $5,000 down a few years ago.
Now you WANT OUT of that 2nd loan. Solution? Go
to a friendly mortgage banker or savings and loan.
Perhaps they will be willing to refinance buyer's original loan and pay off your 2nd TD. This is a 2-step
process, where _you_ actually go out and help arrange
refinancing for the buyer. You still offer your 2nd TD
to buyer at a discount, as in Solution #2, but here you
help arrange to get the cash for him. Example: The
value of that $35,000 house has now risen to $45,000
and the buyer has decreased the $20,000 mortgage to
$19,000. So, instead of $15,000 original spread between the 1st mortgage and purchase price ($35,000
minus $20,000 equals $15,000), the buyer now has a
new spread of $26,000 ($45,000 new value minus
$19,000 1st mortgage equals $26,000 spread). The
buyer now has _new borrowing power._ Offer him that
$10,000 TD at a discount, say $8,500, and if you're
convinced he doesn't have cash, tell him you know
how he might get cash to save $1,500. Go to the
lender, point out the $26,000 spread, and try to con-
vince the lender to write new 1st mortgage for
$30,000 instead of existing $19,000 mortgage!

Net result? Buyer gets a new $30,000 mortgage
to replace his $19,000 mortgage. He gets $11,000
in cash, of which he keeps $2,500, and gives you
$8,500 for your $10,000 2nd TD. It's good deal for

you because you got out of difficult situation. It's a good deal for buyer because he now has an extra $2,500 and has new mortgage on property, a single 1st loan rather than combination of loans. Furthermore, buyer saved $1,500 on indebtedness ($10,000 TD minus $8,500 cash equals $1,500 savings). It's a good deal for lender, because he has safe loan of $30,000 on $45,000 property. Borrower has just saved $1,500, plus an extra $2,500 cash in hand to improve property, if he wishes. All parties benefit in Solution #3.

Let's go to another situation now, and assume you were unable to get cash from the buyer for your 2nd TD! Nor have you been able to convince lender to "up" original mortgage amount! What do you do now? You still want out of that 2nd TD. Answer? Advertise in Sunday classified section of your nearest major metropolitan newspaper. Discount 2nd TD so that it will yield 10%-15% to maturity. People read classified ads who would like to get nice return, better than they can earn on passbook account. They might buy your $10,000 TD for $8,500 or less. Speculators read those columns who may try to buy your TD at a greater discount (e.g., 30%-50% of face-value). These speculators look for deals where someone needs money, and they make efforts to acquire 2nd loans at substantial discounts (so that they can earn super-high rates of return on surplus capital). Do not advertise in small newspapers. The speculators read the big ones. Most subscribers live within 100 miles of a major metro area. Advertise only in Sunday edition, and under classifications such as "money wanted," "real estate loans wanted," or "business opportunities." Study editions put out in your major metro area, read those classified ads yourself, and call up the advertisers. Check out competition. See how much rate of return, and what kind of discount, other sellers of 2nd TDs give. Then you'll know how to make yours more

attractive, and what market is BEFORE you spend
ad money.

Chapter 23

WHEN TO RENT

Suppose you have made a little mistake and it is going to take some time to sell the speculation you bought. What do you do then? Rent it -- fast! Especially if you are lightly capitalized (broke). In fact, rent it below market, if necessary. Always take a survey of similar places for rent in your general area and try to get a competitive rental out of yours. But if you need the money, rent below market.

Don't sign long leases, especially on below-market rentals. A buyer may pop up in two months who wants possession of the property and <u>you</u> <u>will</u> have a <u>tenant</u> <u>unwilling</u> to move! In return for a lower rental, get the tenant to agree to move out quickly in the event you sell the property.

<u>Don't</u> <u>rent</u> <u>furnished</u> houses or income units to tenants. Chances are you can get just as high a rental for an unfurnished as a fully furnished one. There is <u>very</u> <u>little</u> <u>difference</u> in the rental.

Often the tenant who rents a furnished place is a transient and "poor pay." Often he is vicious in using your furniture (cigarette burns, etc.). On the other hand, the tenant who has accumulated a thousand dollars worth of furniture, or more, is a better prospect. He will be less likely to "skip out" on you while owing you rental (especially if you can confiscate his furniture). The tenant without furniture, however, has nothing to lose by "skipping out."

Don't be afraid to rent to blue-collar workers. They are often "better-pay" than their white-collar counterparts. Furthermore, many of them are adept with repairs, etc., and will keep your property in better shape while they occupy it. To save you time and trouble, a deal to keep property in top shape can be negotiated in exchange for lower rental.

Don't rent to families with wild children if you can spot them, especially if you have just spent thousands remodeling your place. Unsupervised kids with crayons can do hundreds of dollars worth of damage in less than one week, making rental income insignificant. Remember the damage they do comes out of your pocket. If the place is a wreck already, no harm done. But don't let them get into your newly remodeled place.

Don't rent to questionable tenants. You are asking for trouble if you rent to people with drug, alcohol, or some other highly dangerous problem. You can place your whole property in jeopardy if some of their acts result in legal trouble. Don't ask for problems. It is better to have your property vacant a little longer and get a good sound tenant, than to rent immediately to a questionable one. Check out the references they give you, especially their last noted address and their employment. No "short cuts"! Check them out!

VACANCIES: ACT FAST FOR CASH FLOW

If you have a vacancy, move fast. One sign of poor management is the length of time it takes to get the "For Rent" sign up. Get those signs up, with your phone number, before the vacating tenant leaves. Slowness in telling the world about your vacancy can cost you hundreds of dollars in rental income. It is a common failing of poor property managers. As soon as you have an inkling that your present tenant is moving, slap a classified ad in the paper within the hour. Don't wait. Contract painters, repairs, etc., same day!

What if you don't have an easy phone number available for prospective tenants or other prospects to call? (Perhaps you are employed during the day and not home to answer the phone.) For $5 to $15 per month you can hire an answering service and use their phone as though it were your own. Do it! They will answer the phone as though they were your personal secretary and you had temporarily "stepped out of the office." You can then call back as soon as convenient.

Chapter 24

POINTS TO REMEMBER

Now you are ready to make "chunks of money" by investing in real estate. However, before you purchase that first piece of property, review these points.

I. DECREASE YOUR NEED TO SELL: Don't be forced to sell quickly. Don't travel that dead-end street. Consciously plan to avoid the "need-to-sell" liquidity trap:

(a) Always have some cash balances, some opportunity money. Everyone should work for the acquisition of some liquid assets to supplement illiquid portfolio commitments. This is a point often overlooked by younger investors. Cash balances can consist of Treasury Bills, savings and loan accounts, listed easily resalable stocks and bonds, etc.

(b) Have more than one real estate holding. You want to be able to work on the sale of a second or third property if your first one proves a little sluggish and illiquid. If you find yourself with a need for cash and have three properties to put on the market, at a reasonable price, your chances of selling one of those three in time are greatly increased. To be more specific, if you are buying foreclosed houses, it is far better to have three houses in the $25,000 to $35,000 range, than one large $95,000 house.

II. LISTING STRATEGY -- Avoid signing long listings. Having a property listed with a lazy broker, under a long exclusive listing, is one sure way of killing liquidity. Increase liquidity with definite strategy:

(a) If you are going to list with a broker, list for 90 days maximum, and preferably only 60 days.

(b) Always switch brokers after the first listing expires and no sale takes place. Never renew with a broker who has failed to perform for you. (c) If the broker wants your listing, get an agreement from him to advertise your property. Let him know that giving him this listing is dependent upon his spending some ad money. If he tells you he is going to put your property in "multiple listing service," but is unwilling to spend ad money on it, don't list with him. MLS is seen only by other brokers. You want customers to see your ad--not brokers! (d) Let your broker know at the outset that you expect performance from him. Some brokers will take an exclusive six-month listing and do little or nothing to generate customers until the listing is ready to expire. Let that broker know you expect him to be busy on the property within 24 hours. Find out, at the time he solicits your listing, precisely what plans and action he is going to take immediately to justify his commission.

III. BUY ONLY BELOW MARKET: This is the most important way of all to increase real estate liquidity. Buy only when you can buy way below market, 20% to 40% minimum. Buy only when there is a need-to-sell present.

You want to buy so cheaply that you can sell below market. A selling price below market definitely attracts liquidity and can be moved much faster.

Don't be afraid to sell real estate yourself and discount your price to the buyer by the amount of the broker's commission you are saving. Substantial discounts often get smart buyers moving quickly, generating fast cash.

IV. GO WHERE BUYERS WILL BE: (a) Do not buy boondocks property. Prepare for buyers before you buy. If no one can see your property because it is land-locked between other isolated parcels, forget it. That's no way to generate liquidity; buy properties only where they are readily accessible.

(b) Buy where many people can see the signs on your property and where they can be easily seen by passing motorists. Don't buy where no one ever passes. Be sure your property has visual buyer exposure.

(c) Stay with highway frontage, buy on the blacktop. Commercial buyers or commercial investors are quicker to act and have the most money available (in sharp contrast to the average family buyer who has, at most, a thousand or two to spend). Don't limit yourself to the average working man as a potential buyer for your property. Even if he wanted to, it is rare that the average man could come up with a significant bundle of cash in a hurry. You will pay more for highway frontage, but you will be able to sell it for more. Don't be fooled by lower "per acre" prices on isolated or land-locked parcels. Buy only immediately usable, buildable property. That means utilities and water either on the property or adjacent. Such property costs more because it is worth more. The liquidity of such parcels may be six to ten times faster than the liquidity of parcels half a mile back away from the road. Furthermore, you will find financing easier on road frontage, utility-fed property.

V. TELL THE WORLD WHEN YOU WANT TO SELL: Increase liquidity on your real estate holdings by taking definite steps when you have to sell. (a) First, spend $20, and have a few hundred $8\frac{1}{2}$ x 14 inch fliers printed, describing the property completely: price, terms, advantages and future potential. Include a sketch or map on the back side of the flier. Using $8\frac{1}{2}$ x 14 inch fliers will stand out like a sore thumb -- far more than the $8\frac{1}{2}$ x 11 inch fliers usually prepared by brokers.

(b) Tell your neighbors. Find out who owns adjacent parcels and drop them a nice letter with the flier. Tell them how this is a chance to increase their holdings at a very favorable price. This source of potential customer is often neglected by listing brokers. You must do some of these things yourself. Don't wait for the broker who takes your listing to do it. He may be retired and just like chatting with people, and enjoy going to the office every day where his wife can't yell at him. You will note all these ways to increase liquidity require some definite effort on your part.

(c) Personally visit every broker within a seven mile radius of your property (whether or not you have listed with another broker). Let them know that property is for sale. Brokers often split commissions between themselves, so listing with one doesn't mean you should ignore the others.

(d) Run small classified ads in your local papers. This is particularly important if you are selling the property yourself. Make certain the property has easily identifiable signs on it before you run classified ads.

IV. GET TRANSFERABLE FINANCING BEFORE YOU BUY! You can increase liquidity on real estate in certain ways after you buy. Transferable mortgage is one way you increase liquidity on property before you buy. The more transferable financing you can lay on that property as you purchase it (first mortgages, second mortgages), the easier it will be to sell. Lay on the paper before signing your purchase agreement. Don't pay cash for property when you can get transferable financing. Make the seller who sells to you eat some of his own paper, taking back some of your transferable IOU's. The note should be transferable to any new buyer at the same interest rate. Insert a simple clause in the note (mortgage, T.D., etc.) that says so.

Chapter 25

BUYING WHAT'S NEEDED BY AUCTION

HOW TO: MAKE MONEY, INCREASE INCOME, INCREASE PURCHASING POWER, AND CUT LOSSES BY BUYING THROUGH AUCTIONS

One of the finest inflation-fighting weapons you can command is the ability to buy through auctions. Action auctions can literally make you wealthy.

That headline made some wild promises. Can you really increase income, make profits, cut losses, and increase purchasing power through action auctions? The answer is _yes_! Furthermore, _everything_ mentioned here is something actually researched and done by your author, or by people known personally. There is _nothing_ in this chapter that doesn't work. Repeat - Every method outlined here is a tested, working method. No guesses. It cost thousands of dollars and countless thousands of man hours to research, compile, and test this chapter and the techniques mentioned therein. Nothing like it, to the best of our knowledge, has ever appeared in print anywhere in the world.

Having this information at your command is going to give you a tremendous advantage, not only over your friends, neighbors, and co-workers, but even over the auctioneer, and you will know his weak points and strong ones, before you are through. After reading this chapter, plus attending a few events to gain first hand experience, you should be well on your way to the benefits described. Before we expand on auction proficiency, let's prepare groundwork carefully with another important analysis.

TWO APPROACHES, TWO METHODS, TO PURCHASING POWER MANAGEMENT

There are two basic approaches to income

management, or attacking the problem of increasing your purchasing power.

The first method is to concentrate on increasing your income, increasing inflow of funds. Surprisingly, among employed adults, few make conscientious continuing efforts in this direction. Best estimate? Only 10% (or less) of the population make it a continuing daily project to increase inflow of funds. If you can increase your inflow of funds sufficiently, you automatically increase your purchasing power. High bracket people are concerned mainly with increasing the inflow of funds after taxes. Small bracket folks should concentrate on increasing inflow of funds by any moral, legal, ethical means. One of these means, one of the best ways, is through action auctions. More on this approach to follow.

The second approach to increasing purchasing power is the more common one. This is the one invariably used by students, housewives, employed persons, fixed income recipients, and many others. Best estimate? Better than 90% use this method. We will call it the "restrict the outflow" method. It is known as cutting expenses (or, in some schools, as "penny pinching"). Most people will spend their entire lives using the "restrict the outflow" method and paying little attention to the first approach, increasing the inflow. One of the prime objectives of The Forecaster newsletter each week, is to help you concentrate on the first approach, to help you move toward a position where you can easily do so. There are many consumer newsletters that tell you lots of ways to work with the second approach (restrict the outflow) - there are hardly any weekly letters (outside of the stock market) that help you to increase the inflow. While this report will help you with restricting the outflow, it will also concentrate on increasing the inflow. Action auctions can move you forward in both directions at the same time. That's good news.

More good news! These <u>methods</u> work - <u>recession</u> or <u>prosperity</u>. They are absolutely <u>great</u> at the pit of a recession, at the bottom. Fortunes can be made in a few weeks. They are also absolutely great at the peak of business conditions, where business is at a very high level, and everyone has lots of money. Fortunes can be made here in a few weeks. This is an important point to remember about auctions - a trained auction manipulator (that's what you will become - an A. M.) can do well, no matter what part of the business cycle he is in, but he can do exceptionally well at the peaks and valleys of the business cycle! These methods are ideal for furnishing property you buy, or getting items cheaply to improve your property so that you can make bigger profits.

WHOLESALE AUCTIONS VS. RETAIL AUCTIONS

You can get almost anything you want at a low price at an auction - often much lower than you would pay anywhere else, including purchases from private parties. But, in order for you to buy cheaply (or cheapest), and sell dear, you must make one important distinction. You must distinguish between <u>wholesale</u> auctions and <u>retail</u> auctions.

Let's deal with retail auctions, first. There are many auction organizations and auctioneers who make lots of money selling lots of goods to large segments of the public at, or near, retail prices. This is not to say you will never get a bargain at a retail auction; you may, but the likelihood is much less than at a <u>wholesale</u> auction. If you want to attend retail auctions for your amusement, fine; we suggest you go elsewhere, though, to make your important purchases. Dealers usually will not attend a retail auction; therefore, take a tip from them and confine your activities (especially if your time and money are limited), to attending only wholesale auctions. You will quickly recognize a retail auction by these signs: (a) high prices for common merchandise, (b) no real pressure to sell, (c) presence of shills, (d) absence of dealers, and (e) high pressure auctioneering. Occasionally, even the most experienced A. M. (that's you, Buddy - auction manipulator) - will stumble into a retail auction. If so, stumble out quickly - you will recognize it within 5 minutes. In fact, you can tell retail auctions by carefully reading the advertisements. If the auctioneer is the owner of the merchandise, or related thereto, chances are it is a retail auction. Usually, the fancier the ad, the more "retail" the auction. Beware of superlatives and flowerly phrases in the advertising.

What about wholesale auctions? What are their characteristics? How will you recognize them? Let's talk about categories of auctions where you are most likely to find wholesale prices, or even lower. For example, think of your friends, the IRS. Businesses withhold income tax and social security from their employees' checks. If the business doesn't cough up the withheld money promptly, the IRS steps in and seizes the available assets of the business until they pay up. No quick pay - up it goes for auction. Same way on unpaid tax claims. IRS moves in and seizes assets, places it for auction after legal formalities met. Watch for notification of IRS auctions. It is quite likely that wholesale prices, or less, can be obtained on much of the material auctioned. Usually, when the IRS places things up for auction, whether it is property, automobiles, furniture, jewelry, typewriters and machinery, merchandise, or whatever, there are no minimum bids. Usually, the IRS auction material will be sold to the highest bidder, regardless of how low his bid is. The sign of a good, wholesale auction, the best kind of auction, is the appearance of lots of local dealers. They buy cheap - for resale - so they don't bid very high, normally. Dealers like to attend IRS auctions.

They like it much better than going to auctions where there are lots of the public who will bid too high. Now you have two more ways to identify a wholesale auction, (a) appearance of lots of dealers, and (b) no minimum bids - material must be sold. Recently, the IRS offered a bunch of large diamonds (5 carats each, and up, etc.) in a Los Angeles auction.

Another type of wholesale auction is often a bankruptcy auction. Here, all sorts of things are placed on the auction block to bring whatever price they can, proceeds to be split up among a bunch of anguished creditors. You may find Cadillacs, mink coats, real estate, brand new furniture (for the bankrupt's office, as well as his girlfriend's apartment) - almost anything.

Another type of auction is often a probate auction. When you go to a probate auction, though, you must be careful to find out in advance whether there is any really good merchandise there. Often, probate auctions are conducted for penurious deceased who had nothing but a bunch of trashy furniture. Also, public competition at probate auctions can get fierce. Much outright junk is peddled through probate.

Another type of auction that can be a good "wholesale" source, is the estate auction, set up by a bank's Trust Department for the deceased. You may find Cadillacs, works of art, real estate, all sorts of valuable and readily resalable possessions (including complete going business concerns).

There is a fifth type of auction that could be classed as a wholesale auction. Here, too, you might find all sorts of more valuable high priced, readily resalable items, including cars, furniture, jewelry, machines, motorcycles, trucks, ad infinitum. This is known as a creditor's auction. When someone makes a loan, they often have to pledge good, resalable assets for collateral, security on the loan. If they blow a few payments, off goes the

161

collateral at auction. For specific items (such as motor vehicles), a creditor's auction can be a good source. Customs' auctions good, too.

There are other types of wholesale auctions, too, but these are the main ones. The important thing to watch for on wholesale auctions is that (a) the material must be sold - no matter what the bid, (b) the auctioneer does not have ownership interest in the material being sold, (c) dealers present, (d) plenty of good items, all resalable through classified, or elsewhere, (e) low prices, and (f) shills not present. For maximum profit, distinguish between wholesale and retail auctions.

Reminder - Concentrate on wholesale auctions, not retail. The distinction is sometimes a little fuzzy, at first, but after attending a couple, you will quickly be able to decide which you are attending.

IDEAL TIME

It is important that you consider the weather and time of year when choosing auctions to attend. They are vital factors. They can double your purchasing power, give you profitable items to buy for resale, or to use for your own purposes at a fraction of usual cost.

Weather is simple. The nastier it is, the better for you. If there is an auction you want to attend, pray for sleet and snow. The harder it is to get there, the less competing bidders there will be (including dealers). Bribe the weatherman, and hope that you have to go by dog sled. When only a handful of bidders show up, things go cheap.

What about the time of year? This is the ideal time of year to attend auctions. Ask yourself, "What time periods of the year is everyone likely to be broke, short of cash?" Answer that, and you will know precisely when to have cash, and when to juggle your time and attend the most auctions, accordingly. When

people are broke, it is better for you. What would
be the ideal auction? It would be an IRS seizure of
a millionaire's business and estate, held on a snowy
April 15 during an electrical power brownout. That
kind of auction you should attend with pockets bulging,
if you have to go by chartering a helicopter! Another
good time is the month of June, when everyone is on
vacation and needs vacation money. Another excellent
time is from August 31 to about September 25, when
Pop needs money for school and the vacation bills
are coming in. Another excellent time is from Dec-
ember 15 through January 15, when everybody needs
money and is busy with holiday, and post-holiday
matters. (Incidentally, these time periods coincide
with the best times that coin accumulations hit the
market.)

Summary. Have cash when no one else does.
Juggle your schedule so you can be free to attend
auctions during best buying periods. The harder it
is to get to it, the more you should redouble your
efforts to get there.

A FEW EXAMPLES

You were promised, earlier, ways to increase
your purchasing power. You were promised ways
to cut losses, and make profits, through becoming
an A. M. Here are a few examples of what you can
expect - late model IBM working typewriters were
purchased at $175 and $187.50. These are the same
machines that sell for $750, new. Furthermore,
there is hardly any risk. You can hock these same
machines at your friendly pawn shop for $100 to
$150 each, even if they are not working. Or, they
can be resold through private ads in the vicinity of
$250 to $325, just as dealers present planned to do.
Coat racks that sell for $24.95 went last week at $2.
Plush executive judges chairs that list for $179 go
for $20 - $40, depending on the condition. A couple

163

of years ago, when The Forecaster began to grow, we needed a Pitney-Bowes "inserter" to automate. The salesman quoted us $1,400, plus 5% sales tax. Within 90 days, we picked up the same model, a machine used less than 30 days, for $400 at a bankruptcy auction.

At another auction, a $1,500 inlaid wood custom made president's desk and credenza, virtually new, was knocked down for $400. You can multiply your purchasing power, your dollars, by a factor of 5 by attending and wisely bidding at wholesale auctions. $100 can buy you $500 worth of consumer goods or equipment; $500 can buy you $2,500 worth of action. Of course, if you attend retail auctions, or auctions where lots of the public appear, you may pay higher prices. Nevertheless, all sorts of consumer goods are also available - arm chairs, couches, refrigerators, ranges, freezers, TV's, lamps, carpet, most anything you can name. Once you get the auction bug, you may never buy anything retail again! $5,000 wisely spent, can do the job of $20,000 to $25,000 in purchases! That is how you multiply purchasing power through using these reports.

Are consumer goods the only items available? No, you can get practically anything you want. A few weeks ago, in a sealed bid estate auction, we became surprised owners of a late model Fiat 124 high speed sports car with a bid of $410! The body had no dents or scratches and mechanical condition was excellent. One problem: When we tried to register ownership at the Department of Motor Vehicles (and pay the sales tax due), they refused to believe we paid so little, as their records showed that model should be worth four figures!

Some of the estate bid cars go at fantastically low prices; particularly the unusual models. Sometimes dealers buy their cars through these auctions, too. Estate cars are often low mileage, often having been in storage up to a year and more, while the estate was being settled. Once you get on to auction and bidding methods, you may never buy another car the regular way again! Since initial purchase and depreciation are <u>major</u> <u>factors</u> in the <u>budget</u> of most <u>working</u> people, these few ideas, alone, can save you plenty. Of course, cars purchased cheaply can be resold privately at substantially higher prices. That not only increases your purchasing power, but increases your private profit-making potential. It is sometimes quite easy to make hundreds of dollars on a single deal.

Car bidding is exciting, particularly for the young person who has only limited capital to work with. There are even better ways, though, to make <u>chunks</u> <u>of</u> <u>money</u> through purposely entering bids for potential profit at auctions. One way is to buy entire stocks and inventories of bankrupt manufacturers at 2¢ to 10¢ on the wholesale dollar. Another more common way is to attend real estate auctions. For example, a few Sundays ago, we watched one A. M. pick up a property on which he could make several years' income without too much trouble. It was a large size, apartment zoned lot, in a high density neighborhood appraised by the Probate Court at $78,400. We thought that appraisal was low, as probate appraisals often are. There were residential structures on the property that could be cleaned up and rented to carry the payments in the meantime. Best estimate was that it was worth about $90,000 to $95,000, marketed in a more normal, cleaned-up manner. This was done by checking carefully on the price of adjacent properties, recent sales data, etc. <u>What</u> do you think the gentleman <u>paid</u> who bid on the property? A mere $57,200! Assuming he could get a bank loan of $40,000 to $50,000, and remarket the property over the next 6 to 8 months (even by selling below market), he could probably double or triple his money! Another friend tells us that he recently purchased some fine residential lots at 20% of probate appraisal! A third said that he bought, within the last couple of years, a large, Eastern metropolitan hotel, at about the same percentage. We have seen probate residences go for as little as $1,500! In every case, these people are buying, not to use, but to make money. Such methods are ideal for working people, as one, or more, projects can easily be handled on week-ends throughout the year. All you need is one or two deals to double or triple your income. Chances are, once bit, you will never buy a house in the normal way, again. A family earning $10,000 a year could, with auction savvy, make that money run like $25,000! Others are doing it, so why not you? Who knows, you may even run into one of us, or some of our millionaire friends at these auctions. If they buy this way, and make money, it ought to be good enough for you to become an insider!

Part II will tell you where to find these lucrative auctions, how to lower risk, safe methods to use on sealed bid sales, and which to use in open bidding. It will give you some devastating psychological tools to knock other bidders out, also telling you how to manipulate the auctioneer and blast the shills. It will tell you how to save thousands in starting a new business, how to avoid losses, how to get the goods moved, how to pay for them with less risk, how to allow for mistakes, how to make private deals to hold bids down, and other money-making info.

PART II

Wholesale auctions are a wonderful way of dealing with coming shortages and increasing the purchasing power of your present dollar. Further, through methods outlined you can learn many ways to buy at 5¢ to 40¢ on the dollar. In Part I you learned how to differentiate wholesale auctions from retail auctions and not waste your time with the latter. You gained an insider's knowledge on how to improve your auction timing. Now you can use some devastating psychological techniques to manipulate other bidders, auctioneers, and the shills whom the auctioneers may hire.

BIDDING TECHNIQUES

As you go to wholesale auctions, you will develop bidding techniques of your own. Here are some to get you started, tested and true techniques that really work.

The first guy you want to control is the one bidding against you. Is there a technique you can use to knock out other bidders? Fortunately, yes. We call it the "Quantum Jump" technique. Let us say there is a particular item you are interested in, perhaps a late model pick-up truck. Three or four people have been bidding on it and the opening bid has moved from $400 to $650, through a dozen bids. You kept your mouth shut all this time. Now there are only two bidders left and it has pretty well halted at $650. It has been advancing in $25 jumps. With "Quantum Jump" theory, you devastate the other bidder by a big advance. You jumped the last bid made, not by $25, but by $50, $75, or $100. Your goal is to put that other bidder in a state of shock. Further, you want to shock him at the precise, psychological moment he thinks he has the truck! You want to make him so disappointed that he won't even have the heart to bid. You want to catch him by surprise with your "Quantum Jump". The pick-up may be worth $1,400 but to the guy who thinks he has it at $650, and is in a state of shock, going above $750 is really tough - especially in one jump. Sock it to him! If you are fixing up properties, a pick-up truck at $\frac{1}{2}$ price might be very helpful.

Notice that you have done several things, they are subtle, but they are very important, each and every one:

1. You used the element of surprise.
2. You used a big jump, a double jump, or a triple jump.
3. You waited until the auctioneer was just ready to call out "Sold!" You didn't get involved until the very last possible moment.
4. You didn't start the bidding on the item, nor did you enter into the fray while the bidding was hot and heavy. You permitted the other bidders to exhaust themselves and mentally make their decision not to go higher before you opened your mouth.
5. You used the element of psychological shock. The last high bidder may take you up one more notch, but chances are, he will not bid 2 or 3 more times. This is usually a devastating psychological technique. It means you only have to participate in the last 10% of the bidding; it works especially well on higher priced items, using the "Quantum Jump" technique. With a little practice, you will find that you can manipulate other bidders, in many instances, to your complete satisfaction.

There is another person you want to manipulate. He's a potential bidder, but not the guy who wants the item. He is called a shill. The shill is usually brought into the auction by the auctioneer to bid up material for the auctioneer's benefit. How do you identify a shill? If you attend a number of auctions, you will see the same shills. Through observation, you will see that the shill is a frequent bidder, but

seldom the high bidder. The auctioneer doesn't want
to get stuck with the material, he just wants higher
prices. Another way to tell shills is to watch the
usage of the auctioneer's key phrases. The shill may
respond automatically, every time the auctioneer uses
a particular phrase, such as, "That's going too cheap".
Or, "That's no money". If you see a certain guy competing with you all the time and automatically bidding,
whenever certain key phrases are used, just assume
the guy is a shill. How do you manipulate the shill?
Very simple. When he is bidding against you, let him
buy the item. Stop bidding, immediately. Soon the
auctioneer will stop giving the shill bidding signals.
The last thing the auctioneer wants is to be stuck with
a lot of a shill's purchases. We call this the "reluctant bidder" technique. Be reluctant to bid whenever
you think you have identified the shill. Auctioneers
don't change shills frequently, so if you go to three
auctions by the same auctioneer, you will know who to
stick on the second or third auction, automatically.

Part I of this report stated that you would become
an Auction Manipulator (AM) by following these techniques, and with a little experience. The third person
you want to manipulate is the auctioneer. When you
manipulate the auctioneer's shill, you automatically
begin to manipulate the auctioneer. There are other
ways you can manipulate the auctioneer. One is to become friendly with him, either before the auction or
afterwards. This sets you up for the coming auction.
You not only become friends with the auctioneer, but
you help him out, occasionally. For example, every
auctioneer has trouble getting certain items started,
especially if they are unusual. If it's an odd-ball furniture piece, or some strange but expensive machine and
the auctioneer can't get an opening bid, give him a
ridiculously low one. For example, if there is a large,
new micro-film reader that you think will go for $300
and the auctioneer can't seem to get it started, give

him an opening bid of $10 or $20, then drop out. If
you do this half a dozen times, and the auctioneer gets
to know you, he will throw good items your way. He
will be grateful. Here, out of the pure charity of
your heart you get these things going for the poor guy.
Even if yours is the only bid, you can probably pawn
that micro-film reader for a hundred dollar bill.
Don't be afraid to help the auctioneer out now and
then, and make sure that he knows who is helping
him. When you have something you are really interested in, the auctioneer will pay you back occasionally
by cutting bidding short, so that you get it at a lower
price than you might expect. This happens much
more frequently than you might think.

MAKING PRIVATE DEALS LATER
        There is a way of manipulating other bidders that
you should know about. This involves sensing who
your competitors are on a particular lot and letting
them know (a) you want to split that lot with them
later, or (b) they can split with you.
        Usually, just a quiet nod or two with a guy who
has been competing with you on similar material will
do the trick. For example, if he and you are fighting
over $5,000 retail worth of something you need, and
he and you have carried the bidding from $800 to
$1,500, you might purposely drop out, with a nod to
him. After all, if you and he continue to fight over it,
it may go to $3,000 and the bulk of each of your prof-
its will be gone, no matter who gets the lot. Immediately after he is awarded the lot, you go over to him,
apprise him of what you did, and why you dropped out,
and ask if he will split that lot with you. Offer him
$20, $50, or $100 extra for his trouble, in splitting
the goods. This will get his immediate attention and
response and, usually, his future cooperation. No
sense just the two of you fighting tooth and nail on
future lots. Let him know, by taking turns dropping

out, that he can split lots with you, and you with
him.

There is another bidding technique you should
know of. Call this the "$200 dropout" rule. It works
like this; if you go to a busy auction, a big one, there
is a certain point where a lot of buyers will drop out.
That point seems to be between $200 and $300, no
matter what the item is. The bulk of the bidders just
disappear. Further, at crowded auctions, the enthusiasm of the crowd is greater in the beginning than it
is after 3 or 4 hours of sitting or standing. They become tired, spend what money they have, then leave.
The likelihood of your getting the best buys then is
near the end of the auction, not the beginning. Let
the initial surge of buyer enthusiasm run its course.
Don't fight it. Let them spend their $200 or $300
early. Often, they will disappear and the tide will
turn (toward lower bidding) in your favor. For example, early in an auction, a late model IBM Selec-
tric typewriter might be $420. If there are lots of
them, by the end of the auction, that same machine
may be bringing only $225 or $250. We have seen
it happen time after time. The less spenders present, the better for you.

Another way to encourage the "$200 dropout" is
to do just that - you drop out, let him spend his wad
early. You can also use "Quantum Jump" bidding to
make them feel foolish later. Remember, all is fair
in love, war, and auctions.

SEALED BID TECHNIQUES
In sealed bid auctions you can often buy far
cheaper. That's because bidders are not openly competing against each other. One devastating psychological technique for sealed bid auctions consists of
simply breaking a psychological barrier. For example,
people think in terms of even numbers ($400, $500,
$1,000). Your strategy? Never bid even numbers.

171

Bid $401, $511, $1,051. Bid over the psychological barrier. This is very important in sealed bid sales. Many times, you will pick up great buys simply by bidding odd amounts, from $1 to $21 above what you consider an obvious psychological barrier. It is very simple, yet, for the risk of a few odd dollars, this technique can often double your chances of becoming the winning bidder on profitable items.

WHEN IS A BARGAIN A BARGAIN?

A bargain is a true bargain only if it is precisely what you want, need, or can resell at a quick and immediate profit. Everything else - forget it! The tendency to buy all sorts of unplanned things will crop up 100 times at an auction. You must defeat that tendency. The smart bidder is not the one who bids on everything, but the one who bids only on those precise items he specifically wants, needs, or can profit from, immediately. Anything else - let it go! You must be stronger than the persuasive auctioneer and enthusiastic crowd. Profitable AM means higher willpower, exercise of self-discipline.

HOW TO ALLOW FOR MISTAKES

Everyone makes mistakes. You will, too. Here is a technique that automatically corrects your mistakes before you make them. First, you must know precisely what you are going to bid on, long before the auctioneer puts it up. That means inspection and compiling a list.

Second, when you have compiled this list, put down the price at which that item would be a "steal". If you can't "steal" it, you don't want it. Now, take that "steal" figure and deduct 20%. What's the 20%? It's your "mistake allowance." Sometimes you will buy something that looks good, but when you go to pick up your newly purchased merchandise, it doesn't work, or it's a cheaper model, or something is wrong with it. You must have a <u>mistake</u> <u>allowance</u>. It is an absolute <u>necessity</u> for becoming a successful insider, a profit-making AM. Make sure you have one!

The third thing you must do is firmly resolve to obey your "steal" limits. Never go <u>beyond</u>! The discipline is good for you. Enforce it! Otherwise, you will become "unglued" in the heat of enthusiastic bidding, and your emotions will take over and carry the bids far beyond your limit, beyond your mistake allowance. A successful AM <u>never</u> permits this to happen. When in doubt, <u>stop</u> bidding. When it gets beyond your predetermined limit, stop bidding - <u>no</u> <u>exceptions</u>. There will be another auction next week or next month, with the same stuff, believe it or not.

THE MOST IMPORTANT SECRET OF SUCCESS

If someone asked us the most important requirement, or secret, of becoming a profit-making auction insider, it would be this: Know precisely what you want in advance, inspect it carefully before you bid, and set up a predetermined limit before bidding opens! Careful inspection and knowledge are the key elements. There is no substitute for precision - knowing the precise model, number, or what you want to buy, and bidding accordingly.

Are you starting a new business and trying to buy your needed equipment at 10¢ to 20¢ on the dollar? If so, you want to know what equipment to bid on at auction. You <u>must</u> <u>talk</u> to salesmen on new equipment <u>beforehand</u>; get prices, model numbers, demonstrations, and inspect serial numbers. Many times, for example, on office equipment, the model built 8 years ago <u>looks</u> the same as today's model. The only way you can know the difference might be by checking the serial number or name plate. Often, the same firm may put out one piece of equipment that is twice as expensive as a similar appearing machine. Only by carefully checking in advance will you know which is

the "high class" piece and which is the "bummer." No
substitute for precision and advance inspection and predetermined limit. Short-cuts or poor discipline will
be throwing away one hundred dollar bills. Precision
and careful preinspection gives you the inside track to
"steal" good buys at 5¢ to 20¢ on the dollar when the
likely bidders around you are not quite aware of what's
being offered. Beef up your advantages by doing your
advance work and exercise discipline. Stack the deck
in your favor through careful preinspection and knowledge.

WHERE DO YOU FIND THESE AUCTIONS?
This sounds like the hardest part but, actually, it
is the simplest.
1. Make sure you have carefully studied how to
   differentiate between wholesale and retail
   auctions.
2. Study the techniques to be used and make up a
   long list of the kind of items you will be interested in.
3. Ninety percent of the readers of this report
   live within a 100 mile drive of a large, metropolitan area. Get the biggest Sunday newspaper for that area and find out in what section of the paper the auctioneers advertise.
   For example, in every Sunday's Los Angeles
   Times there is at least a full 1½ pages of auctions described. If your metro newspaper has
   no specific auction section, call their ad department and find out where auction ads are
   placed.
4. Go to the yellow pages of your nearest metro
   area and drop every advertising auctioneer a
   card, asking to be put on his mailing list.
   Soon your mailbox will be full of the most
   widespread, varied type of auctions far beyond
   your wildest imagination. Your problem then

will not be learning about the auctions, but which ones to choose.

5. Most every major metro area has what is called a "legal" newspaper. In Los Angeles, one of these is the Journal of Commerce & Independent Review. These little papers publish notices of foreclosures, probates, real estate auctions, estate auctions, bankruptcies. (As a side benefit you will find which of your neighbors are being sued.) In an area like L. A., there are hundreds of foreclosure auctions, alone, every month. The legal newspaper is mostly for real estate auctions but, occasionally, you will find boats, vehicles, and other valuables, too.

6. Visit your County Court House. They will probably have notices of Sheriff's sales. Also try the Federal building in your area to find out about IRS auctions. Write the Customs Department of the Treasury for information on seized goods customs auctions. Finally, if this doesn't provide you with literally hundreds of auctions to attend in coming months, haunt your biggest area banks until you find out what they are doing with the Estate goods (cars, property, furniture, jewels, etc.) in their Trust Department. Chances are, they are probably disposing of them by sealed bid. Why should attorneys be the only ones bidding on the deceased's goods. The more bidders there are, the better prices for the heirs! Ferret out that info!

Chapter 26

THE SENIOR CITIZEN

If you are in the last- or third-quarter century of your lifetime, this chapter is directed at you. If you think some folks are sloppy with their financial affairs during their lifetimes, you should see what a mess they leave when they pass on! Unfortunately, people can work many long years to accumulate hard assets and then, after they die, most of the value is skimmed off unexpectedly.

How does the skimming process work after death? First of all, the biggest skimmers legally, are the government and the state. As estates are appraised above the five and six figure level taxes increase sharply. Many times the valuable things in the estate have to be sold off at a tiny fraction of their true worth to pay off burdensome taxes. The second big skimmer is the legal process. Ask any honest attorney and he will tell you what a huge portion of an estate can be consumed in lawyers' fees, court fees, and appraisals. It is not cheap to die these days.

There are many other skimming processes that take place. There can be attacks on the estate by predatory relatives, near and far. There can be hoards of salesmen descending upon widows and children. Often times, when folks die suddenly, valuable keepsakes, jewelry, and other portable pieces turn up "missing" in the appraisal. Substitution of cheap goods can take place when unqualified strangers have access to valuable pieces without adequate security provisions. The condition of an estate changes sharply and rapidly after the owner disappears, and the direction in which it changes is always the same - DOWNWARD in value - as the skimming and erosion take place. Fortunes can be dissipated in a few years due to an untimely end poorly planned in passing.

WHAT YOU CAN DO

There are certain steps you can take to make your present years more enjoyable and insure that the things you would like to see happen truly come to pass. Nothing is so worthless as being known as a "good guy" too late. If you are a "stinker" now, the apportioning of money and valuables after your passing will do little to change that opinion. Drawing down capital is the key. If you want to keep control of your assets and have certain conditions and goals fulfilled, the secret is to draw down capital in advance in an intelligent manner. Most folks who have heirs want those heirs to perform or act in a certain way. Let us say you want to influence some young adults either in the university direction or some career. The time to start influencing them and helping them financially is while you are still alive - not after death when they are beyond your control. If you want to attach conditions to financial assistance, give the assistance and make those conditions work while you are around to see the job done properly, while you have something to say about it.

Gifts of physical possessions to organizations and charities that are tax deductible can be made during your lifetime and the tax money used to make your life easier and more enjoyable. It is far cheaper to give something away before you die than after. For example you may have a rare painting you wish to donate. You can donate that item and make it the condition of the donation that you retain ownership for a certain period of time or until your death.

The idea works out well with real estate too. Folks sometimes donate houses or buildings with the stipulation that they be permitted to live there while alive. A coin collection is another example. Let us say you have a small collection, $500 worth, that you wish a grandson to have. Why not just give it to him? If you put it in your will and it becomes a part of your estate, the estate tax will be raised because of the appraised coin collection. Appraisal fees will be higher. Furthermore, the youngster may have to wait a year or three to get his hands on it. Once he does get his hands on it he may be broke and sell it to a dealer for a fraction of its value. Would it not be far, far better to give it to him now and guide his knowledge of what he has while you are alive?

Conditional give-aways and deductions should be discussed with a tax man who specializes in keeping up with current regulations.

Drawing down capital has other implications for mature people. Businessmen will very successfully work for 50 years to build up a six or seven figure estate and will drive themselves till their last day on earth in continual accumulation. They will put up with harsh climates, long hours, and deny themselves visits to friends, etc., at precisely the time when they have the means to accomplish better ends. In other words, they work so hard at the means that they lose sight of the reasons or goals for such hard work, and their momentum carries them far beyond their original intentions. Thus the means becomes the end as the logical goals are pushed aside through habit.

Example: a man builds up a business worth $550,000 as he approaches his 70's - and yet lets the business run him. At precisely the time when he has more money than he can spend without self-destruction, he is denied the means of using it. The business captivates the people who began it. The only answer in such a case is the intelligent planned drawing down of capital.   Near age 70 you should be drawing down and distributing and spending 3% per year, if your estate is $100,000 or more.   This gives you 33 more years to work off the remainder of the capital.   You will not run out of capital (drawing it down at 3% per year) until you reach the age of 103.   There is only one way to legally frustrate the estate taxman - get the estate used up before the taxman gets a whack at it.

Here is a practical example: a grandchild was recently born in your family and you have just reached your 70th birthday and have a net worth of $100,000.   You would like to contribute $3,000 to insure the kid's start in college.   The WRONG WAY to do it is just leave him $3,000 in your will!   The right way is to set up a $3,000 fund in the kid's name now. By moving the $3,000 out now, you lower your net worth to $97,000 and, therefore, you lower your taxable estate by the same amount.   Furthermore, the kid can draw interest on the money up to $750 per year and thereby (at his tender age) avoid income tax.   You, however, are in a much higher tax bracket.   Net result is that your estate tax base is lowered, you pay less income tax, and the kid is assured of receiving the funds.   You have seen to it personally.   This is much better than relying on a third party to do the deed after your death.   Third example: you may have a net worth of $200,000, all of which is tied up in a building or farm where you reside.   You have recently had your 70th birthday party.   While you do have a sizable net worth, you have no loose cash to do the things you wish. You fully realize that at a forced estate sale after your death the building farm might bring only $80,000 (because of a forced quick sale) - not the $200,000 that it is worth.   Yet you want to continue living there.   How do you solve this situation?   What do you do? The answer is simple: you borrow 80% or 90% of what the land or building is worth, as high a percentage of total value ($200,000) as you can get. Let us say you shop around and can negotiate a bank loan for $175,000. This loan gives you plenty of loose cash to work with and can be reinvested elsewhere to generate $15,000 or $20,000 per year (perhaps in a depressed bond market). The interest generated can be used to offset the interest on the bank loan. Now you have a free-wheeling fund of $175,000 to work with and you can also draw that fund down (withdrawing capital at 3% per year).

The most beautiful part of this scheme is its effect on a forced estate sale. You KNOW that if there is a bank loan outstanding of $175,000 at the time of your demise, that no forced, quick sale at a shark valuation will take place. Why? The bank is going to see to it, if at all possible, that the sale brings in more than $175,000 THEY have loaned on it! The bank will be forced, because of self-interest, to see that an orderly sale near actual value takes place. Furthermore, inflation can have no effect on you. You still OWN the real estate. If money is printed by the bale, the value of the whole place in dollar terms also rises! By the simple act of negotiating the loan you have achieved all your purposes and can now devote your time to drawing down capital and achieving your other goals, whatever they may be. Should you draw down capital for, say, 25 years, (at 3% per year), at age 95 your estate tax will be far, far lower than without the loan!

REVOLUTIONARY THINKING
The idea of drawing down capital at a mature age is completely revolutionary - the idea that you should die with as little of your capital unused as is financially possible! The idea of drawing down capital is completely contrary to what you have been

told by your friendly insurance salesman - the same insurance salesman who goes around setting up large, expensive insurance programs for the specific purpose of paying estate taxes!

Is it not far, far better to utilize your assets while you are alive - and to legally avoid huge estate taxes? Is this not better than undertaking a huge insurance program and exposing yourself to huge estate taxes - and leaving some third party to do the things that you can do better?

Don't get the wrong idea. Estate insurance does perform a useful function when properly used. Insurance is an important and useful part of most financial programs. But planning for living is more important than planning for dying. If you want something done with your estate, get out and get it done now, while you can. Draw down capital to do the deeds, at 3% or more per year, after your 70th birthday. Whatever you do, avoid probate!

Chapter 27

GREAT OPPORTUNITIES IN EUROPE

There are great untapped real estate opportunities in Europe. The outskirts of the biggest cities are virtually untapped for U. S. A. -style developments. Land adjacent to freeways (existing and proposed) can be purchased near farmland-style prices. European population centers have been expanding upward, not outward. Sooner or later the dam will burst and the spillover to metropolitan outskirts will take place.

In Rome, for example, there is no residential housing. Imagine that, no houses! Everybody lives in apartments - everybody! An investor who is willing to work within the dangers of the political society in Rome or other cities would be wise to try placing risk capital in cheap land circling major metropolitan areas, with purchases made on a small downpayment basis with the seller carrying the paper. It looks almost like a sure-win bet if the individual parcel is well researched and the political scene does not deteriorate.

This outskirts real estate is high priced by European standards but CHEAP by U. S. standards. Someone is going to make a bushel of money by buying up land near autobahn and turnpike accesses. Sooner or later these large cities of apartments only are going to have residential developments. Many new expressways will also have to be built. There is no choice in the matter. Those sitting with land on the outskirts are going to be able to call their own high-priced tunes.

The need for money in Europe is even greater nowadays because many stockmarkets have been

declining. When you identify yourself as a buyer,
you will find things easier this year than last.

Servicemen stationed abroad are expecially advised to get off the base and start researching deals.
There is no reason why you cannot profit greatly by
learning the language of the particular country where
you are stationed and getting out to "wheel and deal. "
American troops are not going to be stationed in
Western Europe forever. Put your free time in the
Service to good use. The pathway is clear. Sock it
to them Yankee-style and make yourself a bundle.

Chapter 28

RECREATIONAL LAND

More salesmen than ever before are "pitching" recreational land and advertising is becoming more frequent. Is the outlook for recreational land good or poor? What is recreational land? Usage and meaning vary from person to person. Is the land in question so remote, so useless, that all you can do is put a camper, a tent, or a primitive cabin on it? Or, is it good land, land suitable for a franchised food stand? Is it good, buildable land within an hour's drive of a major metropolitan area, with frontage on a good highway, with utilities, and plenty of water available?

When you ask these questions you discover that the term "recreational" is often used in a different context by the seller. The tag "Recreational" is often put on <u>terrible</u> <u>properties</u>.

A LUXURY

People really can live without recreational land. RECREATIONAL LAND, SINCE IT IS A LUXURY, IS ONLY READILY RESALABLE AT TOP PRICES UNDER VERY GOOD ECONOMIC CONDITIONS. Of course, you can move it during mediocre or poor economic conditions if you cut the price sharply, but that kills much of your profit. Since recreational land is hard to resell "at market" (except under the very best economic conditions), it leaves much to be desired as a hedge. Sure, if you are an excellent salesman and can afford to advertise extensively, you can move it under less desirable conditions. If, however, you are just a private individual, you should realize that only when people are "flush" will they buy

high-priced recreational land good for nothing else.
If there is a possibility of usage change, you may
find it easier to resell under mediocre economic
conditions.   But to resell it for the same usage in
which you purchased it during a RECESSION is down-
right TOUGH!

DEGREES OF LIQUIDITY IN REAL ESTATE
One of the disadvantages of real estate is lack
of liquidity.   However, different types of real estate
have different degrees of liquidity.   Residential real
estate has a much higher degree of liquidity than
recreational land.   So has usable commercial property.   If a good degree of liquidity has to be part of
your real estate commitments, better forget about
single usage recreational land.

CHANGING USAGE MAKES MONEY
In looking for future money-making parcels of
real estate, it is good to keep in mind that the really
big gains are made by changing the usage of the property.   In this sense, buying recreational land and
changing usage to residential or commercial land
can make a fortune.   Is the recreational land you are
looking at suitable for changing future usage?   If so,
how remote is the changing usage -- five years away?
Or many more?   Difficult questions to answer, perhaps, but you must ask them when evaluating recreational land.   If the best future usage of the specific
land you are interested in is for recreation only,
forget it.   There is a lot of no-good land being sold
as recreational land.   Naturally!   It isn't good for
anything else!   For what higher and better usage
are you going to resell the land?   If you want to make
money with it, it is best to buy it with a low-usage
factor and sell it with a changed potential usage.
There isn't much money in selling it for the same

usage in which you bought it. If there is no prospect
of changing usage, don't buy it.

Land with many uses can be readily resold even
under mediocre economic conditions. Land near
major population concentrations has a much higher
degree of liquidity than land 100 or 200 miles away.
For maximum liquidity, find multi-usage land on
paved roads and avoid the boondocks. Stay near
major metropolitan areas so that population trends
can stimulate competitive bidding for your land.
Competitive bidding will add to the liquidity and price
strength of your commitments. Stay away from areas
where there is going to be no competition for usable
land in the future. You want to locate precisely where
the demand from people with MONEY will soon exceed
the supply. No matter what the demand is, if supplies
of land are heavy or if only poorly-financed folks want
it, it will be difficult for you to make big money.
Sure, there will be occasional exceptions. But what
is being presented here are principles that salesmen
are not going to tell you about. These are tested
principles and they work.

PROXIMITY IS MORE EFFICIENT
When you buy real estate you might as well prepare yourself to inspect it at least four times a year.
You will have to inspect it more often if agents will
be negotiating with you. If the land is far removed,
if there is no nearby readily available transportation
at low cost, it may be too far for you to consider.
After all, you don't want to take lots of time off from
your regular profession to travel hundreds of miles
into a remote country to inspect, service, or negotiate deals on your property. Try to stick to areas
within an hour's drive of where you live or large
metropolitan areas within commuting distance. You
don't want to waste 10 full days a year on travel time

alone to work properly with your property. Travel
time and travel expense add to the cost of any land
you own.

Though not impossible, it is hard to negotiate
deals from hundreds of miles away. It is particularly inefficient on income properties. Such expense
knocks down your rate of investment return. Avoid
that trap with recreational land. It is best if you
invest only within established communication and
transportation lanes. Property that is three hours
drive from the nearest major airport is too far away.
If you concentrate on your own area you can spend
more time working deals with less time traveling.

When you are a resident of the area concerned,
you are likely to learn more quickly of new developments than when you are an outsider, or stranger,
or tourist. You must have this vital information to
know when the best time is to buy, sell, or hold.
Long distance properties are definitely second best
to being there. This holds true for resort areas also,
even though the grass often looks greener there. You
are quite likely to see lots of tourists spending lots
of money. Yet, when you talk to the resort operators,
they will tell you, you are missing something. What
you don't see are the other six to nine months of the
year when the local folks are likely to be scratching
around for income. It is best not to buy in areas
where there are no jobs except those generated by
tourism. You need nearby job concentrations. If
you purposely seek areas near heavy job concentrations, you can be relatively assured of higher liquidity
and more future competitive demand for your property.
Job concentrations mean money concentrations. It
takes lots of income and lots of money pushing into an
area to start land values rising sharply. Of course,
land values can rise elsewhere at a slower rate (they
usually do, but you want sharp gains. One of the

nice things about real estate is that time will often
cure many of your mistakes if you can afford to wait.

ANALYZE THE SALESMAN

If you decide to buy, be wary of fancy salesmen
in $300 suits, driving Cadillacs. They would not be
working on commission alone selling land if it were
so good. They would be investing every dime they
had in it themselves -- instead of in fancy cars.
Unfortunately, too many people judge a potential
investment by the outward appearance of the salesman. If the salesman is dressed well and spends
money entertaining, folks assume that the land is a
good investment. It is quite possible that the opposite
may be true. The fancy suit may be on monthly payments ($1 down and $1 when you catch me), and the
Cadillac is quite often leased.

When dealing with such salemen you should ask
yourself another question: Has this salesman personally made any big money buying and reselling this
land (on an investment basis, not on a commission
basis)? Has he really made it big by purchasing and
reselling land that has gone up sharply in value, or
has he made all his money from commissions alone?
Does the salesman really know the area, or is he
more of a salesman than a real estate expert himself?

THINGS TO REMEMBER

If you have some leisure income and don't mind
spending some on a retreat or recreational land, fine.
But recognize it for what it is. Don't let a fine vacation in a remote area get you involved in an undesirable property. Make this your motto: "If you can't
afford the money and time to personally walk over the
land and inspect it, you can't afford to buy it." This
goes for syndications, too. Never buy land you have
not personally trod, no matter what money-back

guarantees there are. Sometimes people know that they are being pitched by a fast-talking salesman, yet the idea of getting something for nothing has such a strong appeal that they purposely choose to ignore the disadvantages.

Chapter 29

BEST BET IN THE U. S.

As man learned to control cold and the harsher
elements, he changed his area of influence, his habi-
tat. Thousands and thousands of years ago the common
centers of civilization were Mesopotamia, Phoenecia
and Babylonia. From these wellsprings of ancient
culture, man advanced rapidly from his primitive
state to one that gave him many new skills. With
these skills man was able to achieve added control
over his environment. As he advanced in the area
of shelter and climate control, he moved to new
areas (i. e. , Northern Europe, etc.).

It is only now, in the past quarter century (and
mostly only in the U. S.), that man has really learned
to control heat. When he learned to control cold
initially, it took many thousands of years for him to
make a movement into a new locale. Yet, in the past
several decades, it has become easy for the common
people in the U. S. , through the most remarkable advances in climate control and engineering, to control
the warmer climates.

Is it an accident that the fastest growing states
in the country are now states like New Mexico,
Arizona, Florida, Nevada, California and Alabama?

When you begin to realize the fantastic advances
that have recently been made in air and space conditioning, when you realize the way the interstate
highway system is changing the country, when you
know of the impact of airfreight and other modes of
cheap, fast transportation, it is only then that you
can really see how fertile deserts are being made to
bloom through aggressive new innovations. That one
of the unsung growth industries of the future is

agriculture -- particularly agriculture in areas where three to four crops can be grown per year (as opposed to one crop a year in states in the Midwest and Northeast). Modern planes and freeways are making trips that were once impossible and aggravating, a short journey and thoroughly enjoyable. As the evils of metropolitan life become more apparent, the search for new areas of profitability accelerates.

Entire scientific communities are now being relocated in warmer climates. Highly skilled, highly educated members of these communities feel they get two to four months extra living time per person per year when they don't have to fight the elements of nature. When you are paying skilled engineers and scientists $100 to $300 a day, as an industrialist, the small sum of 5 to 10 extra man-days in attendance per year per employee can add up quickly in corporate profits -- especially when you add in huge salaries of supporting personnel. Not only are battles with elements being abolished in these newly located communities, but the decades-old phenomenon of commuting is purposely being eliminated. Anyone who has spent 5 to 20 hours of usable time per week in commuting knows what a drain and drag that time can be upon one's personal productive effort.

LAS VEGAS GROWS

A U. S. News & World Report pinpoints Nevada as being the fastest growing state in the nation with the population up 61.4% during the 60's. This is almost double the rate of the next fastest growing state in the Union. Arizona, Nevada's neighbor, had a growth rate of 31.7% and California, 26.1%, on the other side. The same magazine lists Las Vegas as one of the five fastest growing cities in the nation. One million people may someday inhabit the Las Vegas Valley.

Las Vegas, in particular, and Nevada in general, have a severely restricted supply of land. In addition, there is a wild housing shortage in progress right now! Real estate brokers sometimes cut their commission to 3% instead of the usual rate for anyone who will list a house for sale with them. Some brokers are so desperate to obtain badly needed listings that they not only cut their commission, but give a listing client a free wedding and prepare his income tax! Talk about incentive plans!!!

SUPPLY AND DEMAND

SUPPLY: The government owns just under 90% of all the land in Nevada. Of the percentage remaining, a half dozen individuals own sizeable portions. The rest is owned by private individuals and companies. Much of this land has been bought with cash. Those who sold and were paid in cash are now trying to put some of this money back into real estate, but listings are getting fewer and fewer. Often they can find no better place to put it than in the bank. Las Vegas is small. Most of the large purchases were made from 1965 to 1968, and are not yet reflected in the general price level. Much of the housing shortage is being met by the sale of mobile homes which are rather casually situated on lots with utilities. Since many of the folks who sold their land are putting the cash into the bank, Las Vegas is one of the few areas of the West where mortgage money may still be available at lower-than-normal rates!

DEMAND: Las Vegas is the beneficiary of three growth industries. The first one, of course, is legalized gambling. (Legalized gambling in the U.S. takes many forms -- one has only to look at horse racing.) A second growth industry is tourism, and the third, upon which many fortunes have been based, is mining. All three of these industries will grow in the coming years. In the Las Vegas area, tourism alone brings millions of free-spending visitors yearly.

Coupled with a salubrious climate, plenty of water (Lake Mead) and cheap power (Hoover Dam), an estimated 8,000 permanent residents are moving into the Las Vegas Valley every month. It is hard to grasp the impact of this migration unless you realize that Las Vegas is essentially a SMALL TOWN and most of the businesses have a small-town outlook. Certain statisticians project that the Las Vegas Valley will have a million population as 1985 rolls around. For the first time in the history of the area, it is drawing INDUSTRY. This first big influx of new industry is the largest in Nevada history since it became a state.

The Clark County tax structure is presently low compared with many communities, and apparently those in office are purposely seeking to keep it low in order to keep drawing from other states. Every time California boosts taxes, Nevada gets another inflow.

Gigantic new casinos and hotels are already under construction on the Strip and a new airport has been built on the far southwest end of town. Dozens of new roads have been cut in, and a huge new water system to bring water directly from Lake Mead is near completion. Cats and dozers and graders dot entire square miles of landscape southwest of town and new roads seem in the process of being cut everywhere. Companies from all over the world are suddenly discovering that the big gravel pile (Nevada) is full of minerals, both exotic and mundane. Nevada is selling dirt (full of mineral ore) by the thousands of tons at a pace never before seen in her history. Much money will be spent on roads in Southern Nevada in the next 12 months!

It is a fair gamble that some huge real estate firm will discover Southern Nevada and engage in heavy non-resident real estate promotion. Apparently few brokers have seriously considered selling real estate to tourists.

The cash flow per capita (per permanent resident) in Las Vegas is higher than in most any city in the U. S., including New York.

Most of the smart money is already there and more is coming daily. Money that follows the smart money is just beginning to arrive and when it does, its impact will be quick. Las Vegas real estate is a far better bet than the casinos. The next time you visit, take $500 to $2,500 along for a down payment on a small parcel. Spend less at the gaming tables and instead place your bet on something of lasting value. As a sporting proposition, the Las Vegas Valley appears to be one of the best bets in the West. A little sand and desert property, directly in the path of growth, can be highly rewarding, as it often has been in other states. However, don't chunk down large amounts of your life's savings. Whatever you do, don't buy any real estate anywhere, sight unseen and uninspected. This is one of the surest ways to get locked in and lose money that we know of. Make certain that the land you are considering is good, usable, flat, acceptable, buildable, marketable parcels with utilities, and that the town is no more than a couple of minutes away. Such land currently brings $2,500 to $5,000 per acre in one to five acre parcels, with terms around 7%.

Negotiate hard when you find something you like. Don't be afraid to offer 20%-50% less than the listed price. You may pay substantially less! Use the principles you learn in this volume!

Hint: Try purchasing a few acres with frontage on Las Vegas Boulevard South, two to four miles on either side of Paradise Spa. This is future "strip" area, mostly zoned H-1 (hotel-high rise). Last time we checked, there were still parcels with frontage at $5000 to $8000 per acre; small parcels, on terms. Much Las Vegas tourist traffic comes from California. New casino-hotels closest to the incoming California freeway traffic will get first crack at these tourist dollars. That's why Las Vegas Boulevard frontage south of McCarran Airport appears incredibly cheap right now, in this author's opinion.

If this idea excites your imagination, you are well advised to make your bet within the next few months. In fact, during the summer, May through September, it is too hot to be visiting and examining real estate. Best time to shop is January through April, particularly when money is tight. It doesn't take much money to speculate lightly: $500 to $2,500 down and a couple of days footwork with assorted realtors, local newspapers and land owners can result in success and profit.

Chapter 30

POSITIVE ATTITUDE MEANS PROFITS

As you read this book, you were exposed to
certain mechanical and psychological principles.
When employed, as suggested, these tools can lead
you to your first wad of one hundred $100 bills. Fur-
thermore, once you get started, you should be able
to repeat the process over and over again, gaining
strength, experience, confidence, and greater
profits with each transaction.   Your success will be
directly related to your attitude.

To speed up your success, you should know and
develop a successful attitude.   How would you describe the attitude in a few words?

First, you must become as a child again.   A
child is able to picture things.   He uses his imagination daily.   He can swiftly shift his mind from present to past and future without making a "big deal" of
that shift.   Before you can ever create that first wad
of hundred dollar bills, you must be able to picture
yourself doing it.   Inability to picture the money,
your goals, and the precise route by which you expect to attain them can hold back your success.

Second, you must learn to concentrate.   The sad
fact is that few people can concentrate for more than
five seconds on any given subject.   Their minds and
mental and physical being whirl in 40 different directions.   If you can just improve your ability to concentrate for 60 seconds to 180 seconds at a time without
interruption, on any given subject, you will at least
double your chances of success.   In the Far East,
for example, mystics sometimes spend many years
to develop the ability to concentrate for a mere 15
minutes.

No one is telling you to change your life style or give up the things you like. In fact, you will enjoy them even more if you know you can take them or leave them and concentrate when you have the need.

There are, throughout this book, suggestions that may conflict with your present life style. When considering whether you should use them in their unadulterated form or compromise, consider how your present life style is affected by the lack of thousands of dollars. Is it not worth making some small temporary changes to affect far more satisfactory longer-term changes? The ability to concentrate is an intangible asset that no government can tax, no thief can steal - unless you let him. Develop it and make it your servant.

Having confidence, believing in your ability to get your plans into action fast is vital. If you approach this new lucrative business with a negative attitude, you will never get anywhere. Those people who tell us "it can't be done", will never get the job done. Others who come with confidence and faith, and are not smart enough to know why it "won't work," will go out and do it!

It would be easy to spend another 20 pages of this book listing examples of people who actually went out and did it. Like the college student who has 27 foreclosed houses now generating rental income for him, or the many other people who now have two, three, four or more deals owned and many more in process. This book is a tool kit. The proper successful attitude applied will lend power to each tool you use.

You must sincerely try to solve problems and all parties in every transaction must be aware that you are solving problems. The moment you depart from this problem-solving attitude (for example, letting the emotions of greed or fear intervene), your success will be limited. Keep the problem-solving attitude working at all times.

Finally, if you need more inspirational goal power, it is suggested you badger your librarian or bookstore for the works of Napoleon Hill or W. Clement Stone. They can give you that inspiration, even in paperback.

This book, coupled with your own motivating power, can lead you to <u>your</u> <u>personal</u> <u>fortune.</u>

Chapter 31

LEARN THE TERMINOLOGY

As you begin to invest in real estate, you will encounter many unfamiliar terms - terms that real estate "pros" and lending institutions use in daily transactions. These terms can be confusing and discouraging. The better you understand these strange words, the easier your investment negotiations will become.

It is recommended that you study the following terms as part of your educational process. A great deal of time and money can be saved if you can communicate properly with those you deal with.

Abstract of Title: A condensed list of the instruments, rights and liabilities, conveyances and evidences of ownership in the history of the title.

Acceleration Clause: A clause which demands the payment of the entire balance upon the happening of a specified event. The event is usually the default of payment or the violation of a promise in the contract.

Acknowledgement: Admitting in the presence of a Notary that you executed an instrument.

Action to Quiet Title: A legal action to remove any interest or claim in or to the title to property.

Actual Notice: Notice that is actually experienced by the person to whom it is given.

Ad Valorem: "According To The Value." The name given to the Theory of Real Estate Taxation by which real property is taxed according to its assessed value.

Administrator: A person appointed by the court to administer the estate of a person who died without a will.

Affidavit: Admitting in the presence of a Notary as to the truth of a written statement.

Affirmation: A solemn declaration as to the truth of a statement by a person whose religious belief forbids the taking of an oath.

Agency: A relationship of trust in which an agent is appointed by a principal to act in his behalf.

Agent: A person who is appointed by a principal to act as authorized.

Alienation Clause: An acceleration clause which demands payment of balance due in the event of resale (Alienation of Title). The Buyer could not assume the Trust Deed if it contained an Alienation Clause.

Alluvium: The depositing of soil by the action of water.

Amenity Value: The value of the pleasures of a property.

Appurtenance: That which is incident or attached to the land.

Assessed Valuation: The value placed on a property for the purpose of taxation.

Assumption of Mortgage: When the lender agrees that the buyer of a property may assume the liability of a mortgage or trust deed existing on the property, the primary liability that the seller had shifts to the buyer and the buyer would be liable in the event of a deficiency judgment. If the lender will not consent to the buyer assuming the liability, the seller is said to have sold the property subject to the mortgage (or Trust Deed) and the primary liability does not shift. The seller would be liable in the event of a deficiency judgment. Sometimes called Assumption Agreement and Modification of Note depending on the individual lending institution.

Attachment Lien: Seizure of property for debt. Recorded before court.

Attorney in Fact: One who is appointed to act under a power of attorney.

Avulsion: The tearing away of soil by the action of water.

Balloon Payment: The large payment due at the end of the payment schedule.

Base Line: The east and west line that fixes the center of a township and range system.

Bequest: A gift by will of personal property.

Bill of Sale: The instrument used to convey title to personal property.

Breach of Contract: The failure to perform the promise. Also called Default.

Crv: Certificate of Reasonable Value. Used in a G. I. Loan.

Capital Gains: The profit (gain) that is made on a real estate investment.

Certificate of Title: An opinion of a professional person as to the status of the title.

Chattel: Legal expression for personal property.

Chattel Mortgage: A mortgage on personal property.

Chattel Real: Legal expression for a lease.

Cloud on Title: A claim or encumbrance which appears to impair the title but which can be shown by proof to be unfounded.

Collateral Security: That which is given as security for the debt.

Color of Title: A fact which appears to support the claim to title but which can be shown by proof to be unfounded.

Commercial Acre: An acre after the deduction for streets and alleys.

Community Property: All property acquired by husband and wife during marriage except: gift, inheritance, damages for personal injuries.

Consideration: The mutual exchange of promises. Valuable Consideration is the promise to pay money or the equivalent of money. Good Consideration is the promise of love and affection.

Constructive Notice: Notice given by recording.

Contiguous: That which is adjoining.

Contract: A promise. An agreement to do something.

Deed: An instrument used to move title.

Default: The failure to perform as promised.

Deficiency Judgment: The judgment obtained by the lender against the borrower for a deficient amount of money still due and owing after sale.

Depreciation: Loss of Value from any cause.

Deterioration: The loss of value from wear and tear.

Devise: A gift by will of real property.

Devisee: A person receiving a devise.

Duress: The use of coercion to force a person to act against their will.

Easement: Privilege to use the land of another.

Eminent Domain: The right of the government to "take private property" for a public use.

Encroachment: Building over on the property of another.

Encumbrance: Anything that loads or burdens a Title.

Equitable Ownership: That which the buyer receives under a contract.

Equity of Redemption: The mortgagor's right to redeem his property one full year after sale.

Escheat: The procedure by which property reverts to the state when a person dies without heirs.

Escrow: A Neutral Bonded Escrow Depository in which the principals to a real estate transaction deposit all money and instruments with escrow instructions to deliver them as instructed.

Estate: Ownership.

Estate of Inheritance: The ownership one has in the estate of a deceased person.

Evict: The physical moving of a person from a property.

Exclusive Agency: A listing in which the owner may sell his property without the payment of a commission.

Exclusive Right To Sell: A listing in which the owner may sell his property but with the payment of a commission.

Executor: The person named in a will to execute the intent of the person who made the will.

Fee Simple Estate: The greatest degree of ownership in real property.

Fiduciary: The position of trust that an agent has to his principal.

Fixture: Anything that has been permanently affixed to real property.

Forfeiture: The penalty that results from the default of a contract.

Grant Deed: A deed that does warrant title.

Grantee: The person who receives the title in a deed.

Grantor: The person who conveys the title in a deed.

Granting Clause: The action clause in a deed which conveys the title.

Gross Income: The total income from a business before deducting for expenses.

Guarantee of Title: A guarantee that the history of the title has been accurately reported as it appears in the record.

Holder in Due Course: The person to whom the payee negotiates a negotiable instrument.

Holding Property: Having the title to property.

Homestead: The exemption allowed a home owner against unsecured judgments.

Homestead Declaration: If you own a home and reside therein you may declare your home as

a homestead. You have an exemption of
$20,000.00 as head of a family or
$10,000.00 as a single person against unse-
cured creditors. Therefore, a Homestead
Declaration gives no exemption on a mortgage, trust deed, or mechanics lien because
they are secured claims. When a homestead property is sold the first priority
would go to the prior encumbrances; then
the owner would get his exemption. If the
property is sold, the homestead exemption
is abandoned by law, but you may retain
ownership and voluntarily abandon the homestead by recording an "Abandonment of
Homestead."

Homogenous: The same kind. A homogenous population is a community composed of the same
kind and class of people.

Hypothecate: The use of property as security for a
loan without giving possession.

Impound Account: A compulsory bank account demanded of a borrower by the lender to insure the payment of taxes and insurance on
the property on which the loan was made.

Intestate: The event of death without a will.

Invalid: That which was valid but declared legally
ineffective by a court of law.

Involuntary Conveyance: A conveyance to title to
property by order of court.

Joint and Several Note: A note signed by two or
more people by which they have agreed that

collection may be made against all or any of them.

Joint Tenancy Estate: The ownership of property by two or more persons with "The Right of Survivorship."

Joint Tenant: One of the owners of property in Joint Tenancy.

Judgment: An order of a court.

Judgment Lien: The right of the creditor when he records the judgment after the court action.

Key Lot: The least desirable lot in a subdivision because other lots are keyed in to the side of the Key Lot.

Lease: A contract between a lessor and lessee for the use and possession of property.

Lessee: The tenant who receives the possession of property under a lease.

Lessor: The landlord who owns the property under a lease.

Lien: A legal procedure to collect money.

Life Estate: The ownership of property for the life of the owner.

Lis Pendens: A recorded notice of a pending lawsuit.

Listing: An employment contract between an owner and a broker.

Meridian Line: The north and south line that fixes the center of a township and range system.

Metes and Bounds: The name of a legal description that describes a parcel of property by outlining it from point to point.

Misplaced Improvements: The overbuilding of an area. Building an expensive home in an obsolete area.

Mortgage: An instrument by which an owner uses his property as security to borrow money.

Mortgagee: The lender in a mortgage.

Mortgagor: The borrower in a mortgage.

Mutual Consent: An accepted expression for offer and acceptance.

Negotiable Instrument: When a promissory note, such as a mortgage note or trust note, between the maker and the payee is negotiated to a third party, known as the holder in due course, it takes on the legal prestige of currency and circulates freely in commerce.

Net Income: The income for a business after deductions for expenses.

Notary: A state witness before whom certain acts are performed and statements sworn to as true.

Notification of Default: A holder of a second trust deed may keep informed of a default of the first trust deed by recording a "Request for

Notification of Default" at the time he records his second trust deed. This places
the burden on the holder of the first trust
deed to notify the holder of the second trust
deed in the event of default.

Obsolescence: The loss of value from being out-
moded or old fashioned. Two kinds: Func-
tional, inside; Social and Economic, outside.

Offer and Acceptance: The two mechanics by which
the parties exchange their promises which
result in the making of a contract.

Offset Statement: A statement requested of the lender (Beneficiary or Mortgagee) which will
give the true history of the loan.

Option: A contract by which an owner of property
gives another the right to buy the property
at an agreed price during a specified period
of time.

Optionee: The person who received the right to buy
under an option.

Optionor: The person who gives the right to buy
under an option.

Percentage Lease: A lease in which the rent is based
on a percentage of the gross income of the
lessee.

Personal Property: Anything that is movable.

Pledge: The use of personal property as security for
a loan by which the borrower gives
possession.

Points: A percentage of the loan paid by the borrower to the lender as a bonus for the privilege of borrowing the money. Not to be confused with interest which is the percentage paid for the use of money.

Police Power: The right of the government to regulate the use of private property.

Power of Attorney: The authority given to act for another.

Preliminary Title Report: A report on the status of title.

Presumption: That which will stand as a fact until overcome by evidence to the contrary.

Principal: The person who appoints another to act in his stead. Also designates a person who is acting for himself in a transaction.

Purchase Money Encumbrance: Any money or trust deed that is given by buyer to seller for all or part of the purchase price. It is a way for a seller to extend credit to a buyer when he does not have all the purchase money. Therefore when a seller takes a trust deed from the buyer as part of the purchase price, he is not loaning money and no deficiency judgment is allowed.

Quit Claim Deed: A deed that does not warrant title.

Range: A column of townships that parallels the Meridian Line.

Real Estate Owned (REO): Property confiscated by a lender on a Bad Loan.

Real Property: Anything that is not movable.

Realtor: A broker who is a member of a Realty Board.

Reconveyance Deed: A deed by which the title held in trust is reconveyed by trustee to trustor.

Recording Clause: A clause in any instrument which prohibits its recording is unenforceable and void. It does not void the instrument.

Release Clause: A clause used only in a blanket mortgage or trust deed (on more than one parcel) by which the lender agrees to release a portion of the property which is encumbered by the blanket mortgage or trust deed.

Rent: The consideration for the use and possession of property.

Rescission: The mutual release of promises by the parties to a contract.

Restriction: A limitation on the use of property.

Revenue Stamps: Stamps that are placed on a real estate instrument by which the Federal Government levies a tax. Also called Documentary Stamps.

Right of Survivorship: The right of a surviving tenant to the interest of a deceased tenant.

Riparian Rights: The rights of an owner of property adjoining water. The Riparian Owner is entitled to the reasonable use of the water.

Section: One of the 36 squares in a township which contains 640 acres.

Separate Property: That which is not community property.

Setback Line: The distance that a building must set back from the lot line.

Severalty Estate: The ownership of property by one person.

Single Person: A person who has never been married.

Sinking Fund: An actual fund of money deposited in a bank from the earnings of an income property to insure an actual amount of cash at the end of a set period to replace the improvements on the property. It is the most reliable way to provide for depreciation.

Specific Performance: The doctrine of contract law by which the promissor is ordered to perform specifically as promised by the court.

Statute of Frauds: The law that demands that certain contracts be in writing to be enforceable in a court of law.

Statute of Limitations: A law that limits the time during which a claimant may pursue a legal right in a court of law. If he does not pursue within the required period of time his

claim is said to be outlawed. This means
that although he still has the legal right it is
not enforceable in court.   Only rights to be
enforced are subject to the Statute of Limitations.   Therefore, the Trust Note, the Mortgage and Mortgage Note, being promises to
be performed, are subject to the Statute.
But the trust deed is an act already performed and is not subject to the Statute as
there is no further rights in a trust deed
once it has been delivered.

Statutory Manager: The status given the husband by
law to manage the community property
estate.

Straight Line Depreciation: Taking money from the
earnings of an income property "without putting it in a fund" for the future replacements
of the improvements.

Straight Note: A note which is all due and payable in
one payment.

Subject to the Mortgage: No assumption of any liability by the buyer of the existing mortgage
or trust deed at the time of purchase.
Therefore, no liability for deficiency
judgment.

Subordination Clause: A clause used only in a mortgage or trust deed by which the lender "re-
linquishes priority" to a subsequent mortgage or trust deed.   When a first trust deed
is paid, the second trust deed takes priority
unless the second trust deed contains a

subordination clause by which the lender agreed that he would relinquish his priority and remain in a subordinate position and thus allow a subsequent trust deed to take priority.

Tenancy in Common: The ownership of property by two or more persons without "The Right of Survivorship."

Tenant In Common: One of the owners of property in tenancy in common.

Testate: The event of death with a will.

Testator: The person who dies and leaves a will.

Title: The right to the ownership. The condition of ownership.

Title Insurance: A policy which insures title of the owner in the event there is any defect in the title.

Topography: The contour of land.

Township: One of the six mile squares in a range that contains 36 sections.

Township and Range System: The crossing of a Base Line and Meridian Line that fixes the point from which a system of townships and ranges are identified.

Trust Deed: A deed by which the trustor conveys his title to a trustee to be held in trust as security to borrow money.

Trustee: The person who holds the title in trust as security for the loan.

Trustor: The borrower in a trust deed.

Undue Influence: The use of persuasion to influence a person to act against their will.

Unenforceable: That which is not enforceable in a court of law.

Unlawful Detainer: A legal action by which a person in possession of property is evicted from the premises.

Unmarried: A person who has been widowed or divorced.

Valid: That which is enforceable by law because it has conformed to the requirements of the law.

Vendee: The buyer.

Vendor: The seller.

Void: That which is not enforceable by law because it has not conformed to the requirements of the law. Its imperfection cannot be cured by an act of the parties.

Voidable: That which has an imperfection that can be cured by an act of the parties.

Water Table: The depth at which water is found below the surface of land.

<u>Without Recourse:</u> The words used when you endorse
        an instrument to avoid liability to subsequent
        holders.

Chapter 32

SHORTCUTS TO READING REAL ESTATE
CLASSIFIED ADS FOR NEW BUYERS

IDEAL OWNER-USER PROPERTY: Doesn't show
    sufficient income to justify present outrageous
    asking price.

FIXER: A wreck. Katzenjammer Kids used as home
    TNT lab.

NEEDS WORK: Hit by last major earthquake.

FINANCING AVAILABLE: Savings & loan got stuck
    with it on a foreclosure. Try LOW bid.

ROOM FOR POOL: Present owner was quoted
    $23,500 to put one in; heart attack victim.

MUST SELL, NO RESERVE: Some hope here for a
    good buy.

ATTORNEY ORDERS SALE: Acting on someone else's
    instructions, of course.

NEAR TO UTILITIES: Should be in by 1987.

PARTNERSHIP DISSOLUTION: The guys argued and
    fought when they found out they paid too much
    and it could not be sold! Maybe try a low bid.

MINIMUM BID, APPRAISED VALUE: No bargains
    here.

POTENTIAL REZONING: Present owner didn't find
    it worthwhile, or couldn't get the zoning job
    done.

GENTLY ROLLING, INTERESTING VIEW: Tax
    shelter as goat farm, 45 degree slope, boxcar-
    size boulders.

IDEAL OWNER-USER, SPACE AVAILABLE: Last
    tenants skipped out, stuck owner for rent, now
    it's empty! Might make offer, way below
    market.

Chapter 33

MOST FREQUENTLY-ASKED QUESTIONS - AND ANSWERS. MONEYMAKER GUIDES

Q.   Isn't real estate risky at today's high prices? How do I know I'll be able to sell for the same or more money?

A.   Yes, real estate is always risky. There is no guarantee that you'll be able to sell at the same, at higher or even at lower prices, at various points in the business cycle.

The entire strategy of buying distressed property depends on buying it cheap. When you buy property cheap, you can afford to sell CHEAPER than if you paid full ticket retail. The strategy of buying 20%-60% below conservative market appraisal takes the "top" off the risk of any downturn in the real estate market. Further, if you finance 80% of the property, you're only risking 20%. If you can finance more, you're only risking your down payment, pushing more risk to the mortgage holder. Therefore, if you go to buy a $65,000 conservatively-appraised property in a distressed market for $48,000, and you can get an easy $40,000 mortgage on the property - either immediately, or by later refinancing - your risk is limited to $8,000 on a property that has a market value of $65,000. Even if the market value fell from $65,000 to $55,000 in a soft market, you would never have much more than $8,000 at stake, plus a small equity built up. If it were good, usable, rentable property, you could have rental inflow picking up the payments, helping to carry your expenses, and equity while you waited out the market for values to rise and sales to

put in your 35 or 40 hours per week, and grab
your 3-day weekends and vacations, and salary
increases, etc., all your life with no struggles,
no sickness, no shortages, no wars, no unemployment, no problems?! That's absolutely
ridiculous!

Get busy and do something for YOURSELF.
Quit "waiting for things to improve" -- opportunities will seldom be greater than today. Don't
be cutting back. Why be influenced by the bad-
mouth pessimistic comments of those who have
been brainwashed and are now disillusioned with
their naive expectations?! Following them just
sets one up for further problems. You live in the
real world, not some fairy tale economy where
there is no inflation, where there is always full
employment, and ever-increasing paychecks with
healthy Hollywood-TV-style people smiling, and
living the good life forever after. That's ridiculous! There is no such thing as security. There
is no such thing as a one-time investment that
requires "no looking after." Money-management
is a full-time affair, and there are no one-shot,
one-decision shortcut investments. As John F.
Kennedy said (while American destroyers raced
to intercept Russian missile ships in October 1962,
to prevent more nuclear missiles from being installed in Cuba and aimed toward Florida and rest
of U.S.), "We live in an uncertain world." Anticipate problems. Look forward to them, because
people will pay for problem-solvers. They will
pay more for problem-solving skills than for any
other skill you can acquire. When you can successfully solve problems, in any field - problems
that have occurred through the lulling, brainwash-
ing of the general public, you will not only triple
and quadruple your income and capital gains, you
will achieve tremendous sense of real satisfaction.

219

become easier. Yes, real estate is risky, but recognizing the distressed property strategy - buying cheaply - helps eliminate that risk. Further, in an inflation-prone economy, we can be pretty certain (again, no 100% guarantee) that 10 years or 20 years from now that property will sell for substantially more if it's well-selected. In fact, it may sell for substantially more money in a lesser period of time, depending on how well you've done your homework. Don't turn a blind eye toward risk, just use and recognize the strategy that helps you tone risk down to tolerable levels.

Q.   I am finding purchases of bargains in property and furnishings a bit difficult, requiring time, concentration, personal effort. Any way to avoid? Friends don't encourage me.

A.   As you look about you these days and seize advantage of distressed property buys, bargains in rare coins, distressed businesses purchased at bankruptcy auctions, or at 10¢ on the dollar, or for 50% of the price of the inventory, it is easy to become discouraged. Everyone around you is bad-mouthing the economy, the present unemployment, the level of business. But, for the most part, they have been brainwashed. They have been misled. They have been led down the primrose path of thinking that things would always be easy. There is some validity to current popular theory that Americans, indeed, have grown "soft."

Whoever guaranteed anyone at birth that one would have an easy life, with no struggle? The Constitution guarantees Life, Liberty and Pursuit of Happiness; it does not guarantee happiness. Nor does it guarantee a right to an easy life, nor does it guarantee that you will never have problems. Whoever guaranteed that you would just

Again, no guarantees that it would be easy -- nor that friends and associates will support, or even understand you.

Q.   Buying distressed property cheap -- is it too late for capital gains?

A.   Your author foresaw construction costs would rise from $12 sq. ft. to $30 sq. ft. over the last 3 years. In anticipation, I begged clients to put 25% of net worth in good fringe area metropolitan usable property. Property was to be purchased at 35¢ to 70¢ on the dollar on conservatively appraised value in need-to-sell situations. It was to be refinanced, either rolling over existing loans or taking out new loans, during period of declining interest rates. Those who followed advice in the first edition of HOW TO MAKE MONEY FAST SPECULATING IN DISTRESSED PROPERTY by John V. Kamin have already seen their equities increase sharply! No, it is not too late!

Q.   I have opportunity to buy huge potential shopping center, very cheaply, in Nanaimo, British Columbia, Canada, currently about to go into foreclosure. Should I do it?

A.   Probably not. Stick to metro areas of at least one-half million population (e. g. , Vancouver, etc.). Your goal is eventual resale, with many potential bidders. Avoid boondocks.

Q.   Should I buy in changing neighborhood?

A.   Depends on what you mean by "changing." If you mean declining neighborhood (e. g. , changing from working man's neighborhood to welfare neighborhood), answer is EMPHATICALLY NO! If you mean changing from sleepy rural, to fringe-area commercial metro, YES! If you mean changing from truck farm to suburban fringe-area

221

metro, answer is yes. Never buy in neighborhoods where INCOME level is declining, regardless of ethnic make-up. (That risk may be OK
for the "big guys," but not for individual risking
life savings!) When you go look at distressed
property, do not be surprised if brokers take you
into precisely declining income neighborhoods --
after all, that's where the "easy" cheap buys are.
But you want a neighborhood going UP not DOWN.
While it is harder to find many good buys in a
neighborhood going up, you don't need 50 good
buys -- you ONLY need ONE! Another reason
for purchasing in up-coming neighborhoods is
EASE OF RESALE. Main incentive to buy property is to make capital gains. If you can't resell
them easily, with many potential bidders, it's
difficult to make capital gain.

Q.   What are the best sources of defaulted property, property in foreclosure, or about to go into
foreclosure?

A.   First source, your area legal newspaper.
In Los Angeles, one source is Journal of Commerce & Independent Review, 210 S. Spring St.,
Los Angeles, CA 90012. Almost every metro
area has seperate legal newspapers. It's usually
a small sheet that lists lawsuits, foreclosures,
loans in default, new business licenses, marriages,
births, deaths, etc. It frequently contains little
news other than public published notices. Second
source is your county courthouse. Most foreclosure sales, IRS seizures, etc., are posted on
a bulletin board at your county courthouse. If
they're not posted, you must wrestle the clerks
to find out WHERE they are available. Third good
source is the lending institution itself. Foreclosure and delinquent loans are hitting all-time highs!
Get on good terms with your friendly banker, or

savings and loan. If you are in an area that does
not allow branch banking, the loan officer at your
bank will be well in touch with "scheduled items,"
(a fancy name for defaulted loans, loans not current in their payments, or imminent foreclosures).
If you reside in a state that has branch banking,
you'll have to get the name of the man who handles
repossessions, foreclosures, and trustee sales
at the main headquarters of the main bank branch.
Your local branch loan officer will probably not
know much about it. A bank with many branches
employs specialists on "scheduled items." Fourth,
attorneys who specialize in estates are also good
sources, but estate sales will probably be publicized in your local legal newspapers. Fifth, certain auctioneers specialize in probate sales.
Sixth, contact your local state and/or county probate officers to find out about probate and estate
sales. Seventh, sometimes brokers can be a
source, too (but not always). Yes, it often requires one dozen to three dozen phone calls. Yes,
it can require a trip to the county courthouse.
Yes, it means you will have to "crawl out of your
shell" and do things your friends are not doing,
things they know nothing about.

    Nevertheless, if you can save or make
$10,000 to $100,000 on your next real estate
purchase, isn't it worth a little "hassle" on your
part?

Q.   I have a chance to buy several vacant city
residential lots or apartment lots at 20% below
market. Should I do it?

A.   No. What you prefer, or should be looking
for, is in-place construction, or usable farm
land, in production. Remember you want some
INCOME from this commercial, or residential,
or farm property, to HELP you make MORTGAGE

payments. Vacant lots just chew up taxes and interest, and yield no income. The property must be usable.

Q. What are the most important elements in the property I am looking for?

A. The 3 most important things to look for are: (1) location, (2) location, and (3) location. After location, the second most important thing to look for -- the essential element -- and one on which many brokers remain uninformed, is owner's need-to-sell. If there is no need-to-sell at present, it is hard for you to make a below-market deal. Avoid properties where there is no need-to-sell. A third important element to look for is problems to be solved, e.g., an income or commercial property with poor management; a residential property that's basically sound, modern construction, but has been allowed to run down through neglect for 2 years.

Avoid paying full-ticket for properties where broker says, "You should buy this because it shows "pride of ownership." You supply PRIDE OF OWNERSHIP after you BUY it at a low price - you don't pay for P-O-O in inflated broker listings. Don't get it backwards!

Q. My broker is showing me an income property that shows 10% return. Your book says always allow for vacancy, maintenance; but building is well maintained, there are no vacancies. I note on this financial statement there is no vacancy-maintenance allowance. Can I forget it?

A. No! General rule-of-thumb is always allow at least 10% for vacancy-maintenance allowance. Naturally, in many buildings there are no vacancies now. You've been in housing shortage for $2\frac{1}{2}$ years! That is condition subject to change in income properties, which move in cycles. When you raise rents (not if, but when!) you get vacancies, and probably you will get them anyway next time cycle turns or as you replace undesirable tenants. Therefore, you must have vacancy-maintenance allowance, at least 10%.

Q.   Newer building shows 11% return, but I question it because no allowance for maintenance. Correct?

A.   Even new buildings must be maintained. All older buildings, modern buildings, require maintenance and repairs. It can be deferred maintenance (postponed for few years) or can be currently amortized maintenance (pay-as-you-go). One way or another, SOMEONE must pay for that maintenance. Neglect maintaining any building for a couple of years, and you get hit with a big chunk at once. Suggestion: Readjust figures, allow at least 5%-10% gross income for maintenance on 2-10 year old building, higher on older buildings, then refigure net income accordingly.

Q.   You stress knowing what rents competitors charge BEFORE I purchase an income or commercial building. I am considering purchase of income property. How do I find out what competitors are charging?

A.   Simple. Visit your competitors as rental prospect, with tape measure. Survey at least ten to twenty buildings within a half-mile radius of potential purchase. COMPARE values per sq. ft. of space. Then compare them against income figures supplied to you on your potential purchase. Yes, it takes time, but better find out if your potential rents are truly under the market, or currently at market, or currently over market, based on competing offerings, BEFORE YOU BUY.

Once you buy, it's too late to research then! Find out BEFORE you put up any money. General guideline: If your rents, based on your potential need-to-sell purchase price, are not at least 25% below competing offerings in that general area for similar properties, don't buy.

Q.   After going through income statements, my friend wants to sell me a building that, she says, will yield 11%. This seems higher than I can get on my life's savings. Building seems priced at full market. Should I do it?

A.   You buy speculative real estate to MAKE A CAPITAL GAIN, not to get fully-taxable income. Example: A particular commercial building shows scheduled income of $15,000 per year, based on current rentals. You know that similar modern commercial buildings have been bringing 5 times gross income, or $75,000. Your job is to buy a building and work the deal in such a way that you can get scheduled gross income up to $25,000 per year. Then, by selling at 5 times scheduled gross income (5 x $25,000), you can sell at $125,000, making a substantial $50,000 capital gain. You don't buy income properties just to get income -- you BUY them to solve problems, and reinstall good management and raise income, so that you can sell FOR SIZEABLE CAPITAL GAINS. The interim income, while helpful for making mortgage payments, is really secondary to your capital gains goal. Keep your eye on the ball.

Q.   Someone wants to sell me a building at a little below market, where the rents are abnormally low. Neighborhood shows I would have difficulty getting higher rents. The building needs plenty of work. Should I buy it?

A.   If there would be a delay in your raising rents to full-market levels, it is suggested you avoid. We anticipate rent control within 2 to 9 months on a local level, perhaps later on a national level. If you don't have your rents up by then, chances are you may lose your opportunity, be stuck with an unresalable deal, strapped in by rent controls (at a time when no one wants to buy properties because of the rent controls).

Q.   I have analyzed the income flow on a particular property, but suspect that a few repairs may crop up which I have not noticed, nor am expert about. What shall I do about this feeling of insecurity?

A.   When you buy speculative properties, or distressed properties at 35¢-70¢ on the appraised dollar in a need-to-sell situation, make sure you have bought the property cheaply enough to allow 10% of purchase price for unseen repairs, e. g., plumbing, roofing, sub-standard garbage disposals, rusted locks, exterminators, clogged bathtubs and sewers, etc. There are always some "snakes in the woodpile" that you will not see until after you are the owner. Suggestion: Purchase 10% cheaper, reserve that 10% to make unseen but needed repairs later. If you pay full ticket in the beginning, and use up your capital, you'll spend sleepless nights trying to avoid repairs. On the other hand, if you negotiate lower price based on unseen contingencies, you'll have the funds necessary to revamp the building.

Q.   I looked over income-flow statements on property in which I am interested, 10 commercial and residential units, and see no allowance for manager's salary. My husband and I might be able to handle this on weekends, and after work.   Shall I go ahead?

A.   Some allowance should <u>always</u> be made on anything above a duplex for <u>manager's</u> <u>time.</u> Even though you MAY have time available to handle it, if you got sick, or your work schedule expanded, you would have to pay someone to handle it.   On 10 units you should allow at least one week's salary per month for managing, possibly more.   It's work, and even if you don't do it yourself, you put in valuable time.   On 10 units, there should be definite management figure of so-much per year; even a couple of tenants can take substantial time.   E. g. , bouncing rent checks, evictions, re-rentals, frequent repairs, legal negotiations, taxes, and keeping accounts, etc. There is <u>no</u> "<u>free</u> <u>management.</u>"

Q.   My broker complains he doesn't know any properties that qualify, according to the guidelines you set down.   What shall I do?

A.   That's not surprising.   Under these guidelines, <u>over</u> 95% of the properties will <u>not</u> <u>qualify,</u> will seem overpriced.   But you don't need 100 properties -- you just need <u>one</u> <u>winner.</u>   KEEP SEARCHING.   Though brokers are sometimes a source for need-to-sell situations (after you work with them awhile), consider using legal sources, lending sources, too.   Bulldog determination pays off big -- in $$$!

Q.   What is the last most important element in buying property on a speculative or distressed basis?

A.   Resale, resale, resale!   Without potential for eventual easy resale at a substantially higher price, after a reasonable period of time (6 months to 3 years), don't buy it!   If the property has re-sale problems <u>today,</u> that you cannot cure in, say,

12-18 months, resale problems that will <u>still</u> exist, even after you've made your investment and done your cosmetic refinishing and repairs, etc., don't buy it. You want to resell for a sizeable <u>capital gain</u>.

Q.   I am looking at a property two weeks before foreclosure, currently renting units at $80 per month. It's run-down, but everything else in that fringe-area metro neighborhood is renting at $120-$180 per month, for similar units. I think I could buy this 40% below market for the price of 1st loan at the trust deed auction. I could get a new mortgage after purchase to recover cash outlay. Should I do it?

A.   You probably have a <u>potential winner</u> here. Cosmetically refinished, new high-low or shag nylon carpeting installed, new air conditioners, repainting on a soundly constructed building might help to get your rents right up, very sharply. You would probably lose all of your cheap tenants, though. <u>Pursue</u> your <u>investigation</u> and potential purchase here. If you can increase rents by 50%, you may be able to make <u>substantial capital gain</u> upon <u>resale</u>. Don't forget you can purchase fancy new carpeting, sexy drapes, air conditioners, etc., at bankruptcy auctions, other auctions, at 10¢-40¢ on the dollar. (See Chapter on Buying What's Needed at Auction.)

Q.   My broker gives me that funny look you describe when I ask him for properties on which I can make thousands of dollars. He seems interested, but he's asking lots of <u>personal</u> questions. What's happening?

A.   An experienced broker, hungry or not, may want some evidence that you (a) have money or income to wheel and deal, and (b) are a serious buyer, not a time-waster. He may question you. Give him a little evidence that you have funds for income. Don't let him get too personal when he "qualifies" you.

Many brokers are not used to thinking in terms of making a minimum $5,000-$10,000 profit on a property, and appear taken aback. That's a retailer, not a wholesaler. Therefore, your questioning method is correct; it's designed to screen out and eliminate brokers who waste your valuable time showing you properties on which you can't make money.

Continue screening. It's faster, cheaper, more efficient than burning up your valuable time with brokers who have nothing but retail-priced houses to show you. Just as your broker some-times "qualifies" you, to make sure you have some funds available, you are "qualifying" him, to make sure he has a super money-maker deal available, or you don't want to waste any time with him. You qualify each other, but you must not be intimidated by going in with a hat-in-hand, "Please, sir, show me some properties," attitude. It's important that you identify yourself as a specu-lator. You're in there for one thing - to make $1000's. Keep your eye on the ball. Whether the place has a charming carpet, an additional bed-room, is so much froufrou. You buy cheap to sell $1000's higher, and that's the main thing you're really interested in. It doesn't matter that the bathroom has pretty brocade wallpaper. Make some big bucks, and good luck!

CBS TV INTERVIEW

In November, 1976, CBS Television sent in a crew to interview our FORECASTER head economist. The questions asked of our economist were provocative and searching. It is possible you may find the answers are also provocative.

One interesting sidelight: Of the four-man technical crew, the cameramen, three got so <u>excited</u> during the interview they would not leave until they had purchased Kamin's book entitled <u>HOW TO MAKE MONEY FAST SPECULATING IN DISTRESSED PROPERTY</u>! Three out of four isn't bad, but we wonder what happened to the fourth cameraman? (Perhaps we'll make a convert of him later to the hard-money, hard-asset philosophy!)

A CBS Television reporter had been <u>startled</u> by an article in California Business Magazine. The California Business editor had quoted on its front page a prediction by economist Kamin that "tract houses would cost in excess of $140,000 by the year 2000." Why that should have startled anyone was not apparent. After all, that was a very <u>conservative</u> economic projection.

Here are the facts:

	Median Sales Price of House	% of Increase
1950	$9,446	---
1960	16,652	76% since 1950
1970	23,400	41% since 1960
1975	39,300	68% since 1970
1976	44,100	12% since 1975

(For earlier figures, refer to Natl. Assn. of Home Builders.)

FORECASTER estimates that the current median sales price of a house nationwide is $44,100. That is a 12% increase over 1975, and an 88% increase over 1970. As you can see, the prices of new homes have increased much faster now that we are in a full-fledged fiat money economy (gold convertibility of the dollar was suspended on August 15, 1971).

If new home prices continue to increase at the rate of 1970 - 1975 (the more conservative figure) and increase 78% every five years, here is what you'd have:

1980	$66,024
1985	100,920
1990	186,346
1995	313,061
2000	525,943

Using only the statistics for the 1970-1975 period, it would be possible to project a median sales price for new homes of $525,943 by the year 2000.

However, as any good economist will quickly point out, the 1970-1975 period may have contained some unusual circumstances, and therefore it would be better to look at the trend rate in home prices over a longer period of time.

How about using a quarter century of research? Okay -- from 1950 - 1975 the increase in home prices was 416%. Using the 1975 median price figure of $39,300, ignoring 1976's unusually high rate of increase, you would still get a new home priced at $166,488 by the year 2000 -- using figures that go back one quarter century.

That still seems awfully high. Suppose we take a lengthy period in between -- not a five-year period and not a quarter century period, but a long enough period of recent history to be sure we are in tune with modern trends and, at the same time, a span long enough to iron out mere aberrations in the market place. How about the period 1960-1975? New home prices increased from $16,652 to $39,300, an increase to 236% in 15 years. (Again, we conservatively ignore the median sales price of 1976 as being too recent to be valid over a long period of time, even though the 1976 increase was substantial.) Using the figures from 1960 - 1975, by 1990 your median sales price of a new home would be $92,748. From 1990 - 2000, the price would increase by another 90.7%, for a sales price in the year 2000 of $176,870.

The projections made look astonishingly high. Therefore, to satisfy our own peace of mind, FORECASTER, being conservative, arbitrarily reduced them significantly -- in the event that gold-backed money once again became available to help stabilize prices and in the event that one or two depressions intervened. So the figure of $140,000 was projected when the CBS TV interviewer asked your economist what a new house would cost in the year 2000. While they thought that figure was very high, as you can see by the data being researched by the FORECASTER, that figure appears way low.

In coming issues the FORECASTER may give you some figures on what a new car will sell for in the year 2000, and the price of other commonly-purchased items. You may be surprised at our findings.

HELPFUL CONCLUSIONS - WAYS TO PROFIT

Looking at the limited historical data available, it is quite clear that it would be rather unrealistic to expect substantially lower average home prices over the near term, medium term, or long term.

From 1975 through 1976, our projections show home prices increasing at a rate of 1% per month, estimated, a rate far faster than the 26 years of historical data used. Even by seeking to isolate short-term statistical fluctuations in the price of a home, it becomes crystal clear in which direction the trend is carrying, namely any downturn would likely be limited to a short period of time before prices resumed their climb.

FEARS & THE FOOLHARDY - WHO WILL PLAY, & WHO WILL PAY?

For the family to avoid the acquisition of housing, for the family to avoid the "saving up" process for a down payment, for the family to opt instead for a "good time" while they rent, and to postpone their house purchase for 10-15 years, would seem foolhardy. Not only foolhardy, but exceptionally costly. Perhaps to the tune of $40,000 - $100,000!

By the same token, for the young retired person to sell out and go on a rental schedule would likely be very costly. If he wishes to change locations, he might be wise to take advantage of the tax law deferral, selling his old residence, and buying a new one in his new preferred location within a year.

And for the single person to avoid purchase of a home, duplex, triplex or apartment building for the sake of several new cars and a lot of fancy vacations, and to avoid some "ribbing", such avoidance of house purchase for fleeting reasons would also appear foolhardy and extremely costly.

Please don't misinterpret this. Your economist is not suggesting that, anyone get purposely over-extended to acquire housing. What is being suggested, however, it a LOOK at the LONG view, the long term TREND, looking back a quarter century, looking ahead a quarter century and fitting that historical data into your personal long-term perspective.

Whether the last quarter century's trends will
continue at a higher rate, at a lower rate or about
the average rate, _cannot_ be predicted. What does
appear clear, however, is that any drop in the price
of housing should be limited to a short period of
time; that such _drops_ are the _exception_ rather than
the rule. Those who buy during such weak periods,
when housing prices are off, or the need-to-sell is
apparent, stand to make a good deal of _profit._

Even many of those who blunder and overpay for a
house have sometimes found to their joy that the _com-
bination_ of no-rent-payments, and the increase in
the price of housing, has bailed them out, to their
good fortune!

CBS INTERVIEW: QUESTION AND ANSWER SESSION

Q.   Are houses overpriced?

A.   The average builder's and developer's profit
runs 5% to 20% on new houses. The other 80% to
95% is cost of land, labor, materials, and appliances.
If there is a real estate commission involved, it can
run 6% or so. In reality, what you are asking, since
commissions and developer's profits have _not_ changed,
is: "Is the cost of land, labor and materials overpriced?"

I don't think, if you talk to a plumber or electrician
or carpenter, you will get much agreement that _they_
are overpriced. Regarding land, people want to live
where the _jobs_ are, which uses up the available land,
which bids up the price of any usable remaining land.
Therefore, if one piece of land became overpriced,
it would not sell, while a lower-priced adjacent piece
might. So you can't really say that land is overpriced.

Regarding the cost of materials for building, they
are not out of line with the rest of our economy, which
has had inflation rates from 4% per year to 12% per year
over the past 4 years. So the price of new construction
and new houses today is about in line with the rest of
the economy.

Q. Young families are being priced out of the housing market today, are they not?

A. Yes. People without savings have always been priced out of the housing market. Until they learn to build savings, it is irresponsible to expect other taxpayers, through government, to subsidize their entry into housing. No subsidy can be made available to young taxpayers without first taking it from other taxpayers. While we have subsidized Vets and others, to whom we felt a moral obligation in the past, the tax burdens imposed by Washington forcibly are now working against shifting subsidies to one class at the expense of another segment of the working class.

Q. How should the young family proceed in order to get a house?

A. First, they'll have to get some money for a down payment. If they can't save it themselves, they'll have to ask Mom, Pop, or Aunt Tillie. What they don't have, they'll have to borrow, given the unwillingness of other taxpayers to subsidize them.

Q. But suppose they can't borrow? Suppose they already have too many payments to pay back?

A. The second biggest outflow of funds in any family's income is the auto. You have witnessed a trend in the last two decades where young families may spend as much as $200 a month or more on their car payment. Many will get married, buy a $7000 car, finance it so that it costs them $11,000 by the time they get the interest paid, plus another $1000 or $2000 for insurance. Naturally they'll want new furniture when they're married, used furniture won't do. That's at least another $100 per month more at retail prices, plus 18% financing charges. By the time they get it paid off, it will be "ratty" and they'll want more new furniture. They'll need other appliances, too.

And, after all, if they're just married, they'll want to take lots of trips, stay in nice places, with new clothes, Add another payment each for travel, vacations, lodging, clothes, luggage, and plenty of eating out.

The answer is, of course, savings, before expenditures, a good used car bought for cash, not the car payment merry-go-round, at least six months' income in the bank before marriage or shortly thereafter, and possibly even some (a minimal amount of) good-value used furniture bought for cash. The trips, fancy clothes and vacations really ought to be postponed if they're serious about buying a house, until after they're in and on their feet.

This is the alternative to being priced out of the housing market and paying rent for the first 5, 10, or 20 years of their marriage on an expensive apartment.

The sooner they get in their house, the better. The sooner they can get off the monthly payment merry-go-round, the better for them. And that's the answer. Not easy, but that's the answer.

Q. But new houses are so overpriced, It's hard to find anything below $50,000 today. And any kind of nice house, with three or four bedrooms, can easily run $70,000. How can young couples afford those prices?

A. They can't. It's that simple. But who ever chiseled in rock that young couples should be able to afford the very best new house in their 20's? Chances are their parents couldn't, either, so why should they? The expectation is naive. In fact, in Europe today, the average working man may never own a house, nor ever hope to. He just can't make enough money. If you go to buy a house in Europe,

you may have to have one-third down, and, if you can
get financing at all, you may have to pay back the
entire amount in 8-10 years. Things are pretty good
here, compared to that.

Sure, the young couple may have to accept used
housing, but that's great. After World War II, with
a comparable housing shortage, many folks bought
shell homes, unfinished homes, for the price of the
lot and the outside framework, and did the interior
finishing themselves. If they didn't have the money,
they moved in with Mom and Pop (that's a tough alternative) until they did have the money. The very
difficulty of the situation probably forced them to
save better and faster than they would have if things
were as easy as they are today.

Let's face it. Lots of people in their teens and
twenties blow their entire salary on their car and
themselves, in the most selfish way possible, at the
same time they prevent themselves from owning a
house. Yet, if they were able to buy that house
sooner, they might clearly be able to afford better
things for themselves, and their families; faster,
better, more profitably.

Q. Are you saying then, that young families
should first, look for used housing, second, build
savings, and third, buy used items for cash, and
live as inexpensively as possible before they get
their house, rather than buying a new one?

A. Yes. Forget the fancy wheels, the fancy vacations, and the fancy apartment. If husband and wife
both work, they'll get there even faster. The house
is probably a family's biggest investment (and usually
their best). It's really a bit shortsighted not to plan

for it, prepare for it, acquire it more seriously, and benefit from it as early as possible, without expecting other taxpayers or credit lenders to make up the difference for their lack of responsibility. I'm simply pointing out that the best source for helping them is themselves. And I'm trying to help them help themselves.

Q. What about prople who have been selling a house in the past, making a profit, buying another, making a profit, buying another, etc.? Will they be able to do this so easily in the future?

A. I think there is a good chance the unwary may be caught at one point in the cycle. As our inflationary economy proceeds, as easy money disappears, as costs rise, the business cycle gets wilder, fluctuates more. It is possible, if they go to sell at one particular part of the business cycle, they may find themselves in a position where they can't sell a high-priced house for 6 months or so. In other words, as the business cycle fluctuates, houses will go up sharply, drop sharply, go up even higher, drop again, and there will be periods of rough sailing in the interim. Washington has never been able to outlaw or outlegislate the business cycle. Those who are buying should keep an emergency reserve of 6 months' income. It is unrealistic to expect other taxpayers to bail them out of every emergency situation (and that includes builders, too.)

Q. What will be the price of a three-bedroom average tract home in the year 2000?

A. I predict that the average three-bedroom tract house, nothing fancy, maybe not even with a garage, average neighborhood, will sell for $140,000 by the year 2000. In fact, that estimate may be far too conservative. Right after World War II, you could

buy a frame or brick two-bedroom or three-bedroom
home for $4,500 - $6,000. In fact, many people did.
So today's estimate may prove too conservative for
an economy that has inflation rates from 4% to 12%
per year.

Q. Who can afford today's housing?
A. Fewer and fewer people. It's ironic that the
wage earner making $8,000 per year in 1973 might
have looked at a $30,000 house, one for which he
qualified at the time, and passed it up. Today that
same wage earner making $11,000 per year may be
looking at the same house, now priced at $50,000 and
may not qualify (because of the higher price and the
bigger payments due to higher interest rates). His
down payment may have to be substantially larger,
money he has not been able to save in the last three
or four years.

Q. Who will live in private housing by the year
2000, and where will the rest of us live?
A. I don't agree with those who see the trend
toward a larger percentage of the population moving
into multi-family housing. I think the single family
dwelling will continue to play an important role in
the lives of families who want privacy, individuality,
and a place to store their own possessions. In varying degrees, much of this is not available in apartment housing or multi-family housing. Therefore,
I would expect single family ownership to continue,
desirable for a large segment of the population, and
continue to be the form of housing most preferred
and most purchased by most working people.
On the other hand, those young couples who do
not have the discipline to build savings, to build
down payments, who insist on fancy vacations and

multiple cars and new furniture before they buy their
house -- those folks will be priced out of the single
family housing market. Chances are, they will have to
rent for many years while they try to build savings at
a slow rate. The more rent they pay, the less savings,
and therefore they may be priced out of the housing
market for years to come.

I foresee a trend that's already in existence, the
trend toward more square footage of usable housing on
smaller lots, as land gets more valuable. This may
mean more two-story houses, more houses with base-
ments, as attempts are made to get more usable living
space onto a smaller, more valuable lot.

Q. What is the percentage of annual income spent
on a home? What percentage of annual income do you
see spent on a home or housing in the future?

A. In the past, it has been traditional to figure
about 25% of one's annual income for a home. However,
since the prices of land, labor and materials are increasing, while personal savings are not keeping pace, and
while the housing industry does not have easy money
available, I see individual housing prices increasing at
a faster rate. This may mean that a larger percentage
of annual income may be spent on the house payment.
The trend in personal property taxes is also toward
higher and higher levels. This may soak up more of
one's average annual income. Kamin's law states that
"The trend of total taxation is always upward", and
since inflation pushes most of us into higher and higher
tax brackets, the amount of take-home pay left over
continues to shrink as a proportion of the total paycheck.
Therefore, a higher percentage of annual income may
be spent to own and maintain a home in the future,
possibly more in the range of 33% to 36% of annual income.

Q. What possessions must be given up to own a home today?

A. I recently saw a man who had been laid off from his $8,000 per year job. He had his house payment, a new car payment, a new truck payment, a motorcycle payment, and a lot of other payments. I think folks who want housing are going to have to choose between a number of other payments and that housing. Perhaps they'll have to choose to own one or two economical used cars in order to obtain their housing, or to buy good used furniture, or to postpone some of the fancy free-spending vacations and wardrobe sprees.

Q. What attitudes are going to have to change in order to adjust to higher housing prices and costs?

A. The first attitude is that towards saving. Savings get people into housing, and those who wish to get into housing will have to learn to save. That will mean a fiscal discipline that is <u>not</u> high on everyone's priority list today. Those who can't build this discipline will not be able to save, and will be doomed to renting. Therefore, the attitude towards savings must change on an individual basis. How else can they build the down payment? It is these save <u>savings</u> that enable the <u>lending</u> institutions to make <u>mortgage</u> loans for new construction. If mortgage money is to be made available, it must come through personal savings, which makes industry thrive. Without these savings available, without this capital available, prices will go higher than if people build up their savings.

Chapter 34

HOW TO KEEP ONE STEP AHEAD

Much of this How To Make Money... book is fresh,
new information that can help you become successful
in real estate. Insights contained in this book can
help you jump months ahead of many "real estate
experts". Think of this book as a "tool kit". But
just the knowledge contained here is not enough. The
real estate markets are ever-changing.

Good timing is profitable. The real estate markets,
like any other markets, are constantly changing and new
developments are always occurring. Real estate,
especially usable improved property, has a long term
uptrend. But there are temporary downtrends, and
there are periods where sleepers exist and more bargains are to be found. While the information in this
book is dynamic and can help you achieve above-average
success, you may want to go one step further --- to
gain even greater profits. How should you proceed?

The FORECASTER is a weekly newsletter which
is edited and published by the author of this book. Many
real estate professionals consider the FORECASTER a
normal necessary business expense and useful tool, as
do many real estate private investors. The FORECASTER
moneyletter has been a fantastic success for one reason -
the FORECASTER is well worth the money, and much,
much more. The FORECASTER moneyletter is an
exciting new experience, that adds to the security of
your strategy, and helps you achieve knowledge and
recognition as a person who knows his subject well.
Many readers find the FORECASTER a tremendous
profit-making help. A good portion of each FORECASTER
moneyletter is devoted to analyzing the future, what lies
ahead!

Originated, constructed, and written, by a full
time university-trained economist who specializes in
areas outside the stock market, outside the commodity

243

futures markets, you'll see retail and wholesale markets analyzed, for financiers, speculators, investors. Projections, buy and sell ideas, to help maximize profit, plus analyses of sleepers and bargains, this is what you'll find in the weekly FORECASTER moneyletter. You'll also see specific data on estimated risk factors versus possible projected returns.

Get exciting economic forecasts, personal financial checklists, discover new and unusual speculations, as well as scientifically-tested business methods. Get personal tax and money strategy, as well as opportunities in real estate.

In addition, the FORECASTER covers opportunities in coins, guns, property management, and occasionally such exotic fields as diamonds, art, antique cars, etc. The FORECASTER moneyletter has been helping clients reach financial success for over fifteen years and is the recipient of many awards!

Where else could you get all of that information on your desk each week in one weekly newsletter? Foresight can be priceless.

If you're really interested, this is your chance, your opportunity. The time will never be better! FORECASTER members tread a giant step ahead of the crowd and they know it. You are invited to join them.

VALUABLE COUPON

Special introductory offer for new readers only. Discover the FORECASTER -- the weekly moneyletter for practical people who sincerely want to make money outside the stock markets, outside the commodity markets. Coupon entitles the purchaser of this book to eleven $3.95 current issues of the FORECASTER for only $28.00 ($47.45 value, save 41%). Dept DB.

OTHER FORECASTER PUBLISHING CO. BOOKS
AND BOOKLETS

<u>"POWER SECRETS TO FAST MONEY"</u> - A fresh new 1977 look at the best techniques and methods you can use now in any economic period to increase your income and accumulate wealth FAST. No matter what your interests, no matter what your money game, you can benefit by discovering the secrets to fast money. The grand master of auctions, foreclosures, and negotiations reveals his most valuable secrets on how you can buy below even wholesale - and sell higher. Valuable for businessmen, executives, anyone who is interested in making money. $10.00

<u>"HOW TO MAKE MONEY IN COINS"</u> - By John Kamin. Latest, freshest, most exciting, 286 pages -- reveals in depth insider functions for 1977 coin market. Ideas others called "TOO HOT TO HANDLE". Dealers, collectors, speculators, anyone - beginner to professional - will find fresh interesting ideas. Over 200 specific recommendations - S-Mint & O-Mint dollar stories. Let's you in on best buys, worst holdings. Strategies for 100% profits, 17 Guidelines for making big money!!! 165 "insider topics" covered as never before!!! How to Profit even in Bad Markets. No other coin book like <u>"HOW TO MAKE MONEY IN COINS"</u>!!!!! $15.00

<u>"HOW TO BUY 3-4 YEAR OLD CARS AT $200 AND LESS - HOW TO BUY A NEW CAR AT LOWEST POSSIBLE PRICES - CLASSIC CARS FOR FUN AND PROFIT"</u> - Read for success in cutting second major category of yearly dollar outflow (auto, maintenance, upkeep, insurance, and purchase expense). Discover how to buy low-cost transportation with no depreciation, how to save $200 to $600 on a new car in addition to normal discounts, and how antique cars can be resold at big profits. $5.00

"BEST HOPE FOR THE YOUNG INVESTOR TO BE-COME FINANCIALLY INDEPENDENT AND WEALTHY"
- Prepared, researched and directed especially for
the young investor whose capital is very limited and
to whom few people provide much help. It is shown
that this young investor must first destroy a commonly
held attitude regarding investments and what to purchase. $2.50

"HOW TO RETURE IN YOUR FORTIES FINANCIALLY INDEPENDENT"
- Zeros in on the young investor, from
age 22 to 35, in the hope of helping him or her become
financially independent. These years are the most
important as far as building capital is concerned. Learn
why some people are more successful than others. $3.00

"HYPERINFLATION - HOW YOU CAN COME OUT AHEAD AND YOUR PERSONAL FINANCIAL SUCCESS PROGRAM"
- Hard-hitting, no-nonsense, non-techni-
cal suggestions! What's ahead, what to do, how to profit
from coming trends. Also what to do in a highly inflationary period; how to insure that you profit from it.
$5.00

"IMF - ENGINE OF INFLATION - HOW YOU CAN SURVIVE AND PROFIT"
- Fresh new look at future
world economy and its effects on your life style. You
will explore the making of the coming international
crisis -- how it all began -- how we got into this mess --
where we will go from here -- how you can profit. If
you can follow the strategies contained in this fresh new
look at the current and expected changes to come, you
will be the winner when massive shifts of wealth occur.
Here's your chance to understand international economics,
discover behind-the-scenes activity, and learn how to
profit from your knowledge, all in one sitting. $5.00

HOW TO ORDER: These books are all available to you through THE FORECASTER. Please add 75¢ per book to cover the cost of postage and handling. Payment must accompany order. California residents, please add 6% sales tax. Send your order to:

THE FORECASTER
19623 Ventura Blvd.
Tarzana, CA 91356

ABOUT THE AUTHOR
JOHN V. KAMIN

For the last 14 years, John Kamin has been editor of THE FORE-CASTER, one of the world's largest weekly coin newsletters. John Kamin was one of the first members of the teletype circuit, with years of numismatic experience. Kamin gets $300 an hour for numismatic consultations. — now available to you in one dynamic book. **"How to Make Money in Coins"** reveals many untold secrets accumulated over the years by hard coin research from one of the leading experts in the field. Kamin is author of the books.

Power Secrets to Fast Money
How to Make Money Fast Speculating in Distressed Property
How to Retire in Your Forties Financially Independent
Best Hope for the Young Investor to Become Financially Independent and Wealthy
The Detroit Insider — How to Buy Cars at Lowest Possible Prices
Hyperinflation — How You Can Come Out Ahead and Your Personal Financial Success Program, now in its 4th Printing (co-author)

Kamin studied economics and finance at Catholic University, University of Chicago, DePaul University, and the National University of Mexico. The internationally renowned economist received instant fame in 1967 with predictions of the British pound devaluation. He predicted the 1974 recession two years in advance! Clients throughout the world have written to THE FORECASTER thanking Kamin for their newly-discovered and enriched life-styles.

The record of John Kamin and THE FORECASTER weekly newsletter proves that his methods can push you way ahead in coin success, whether you have been in numismatics for years or are a beginner ready to build your fortune.